# Thoughts on the Origin and Evolution of (Artificial) Intelligence

By Kristiyan Kirchev

**Thoughts on the Origin and Evolution of (Artificial) Intelligence**

**Copyright © January 2005 – September 2020 by Kristiyan Kirchev**

**ISBN:** 9798682146314
**Imprint:** Independently published

*At the beginning of biological life - the first cell appeared, and it joined with another, and they made an organism.*
*At the beginning of cyberspace - the first computer appeared, and it was networked with another, and they made a network.*

*Multiple cells organized themselves in an interrelated, intelligent system, and their organization was called consciousness.*
*Multiple computers were organized by Man in a co-related, programmed system, and the programming allowed multifunction.*

*Organized and Conscious Biological cells began to operate the networked, programmed computers to manifest themselves. Ideas poured from the cell organisms into the networked silicon chips, and consciousness crossed over from digital biology to digital electronics.*

*Consciousness rises from intelligent forms, and multiple cells equal multiple computers; like multiple networking computers equal cyberspace, multiple cells equal consciousness, and consciousness equals information.*

# Contents

# Foreword

In 1997 I wrote a Cyberpunk manifesto, which was somewhat revolutionary for its time, so much so that after publishing it on an internet site, it got copied, translated, and republished in over seven languages from likeminded people the world over.

That was really something, yet I've always liked to think a lot and write a little. It goes as far back as the times when teachers at elementary school would scold me for being a "wooden philosopher" (some sort of a Bulgarian idiom indicating someone who thinks and talks too much about impractical matters). I guess teachers didn't like me speculating and theorizing upon funnel-fed educational material. All, but my high-school literature teacher, who wanted to me to stay after class and discuss my interpretations of de Cervantes' Don Quixote. It is for that Literature teacher who encouraged me to stick with thinking and writing.

In the years of the early internet - social networking forums and world-wide-web, all taking over the world - I wrote most of my works on-line and on the topics of them emerging technologies which shaped society and changed the way we function, as human-beings, to date.

In 2010 I collected my writings since 2005 and collated them in a compilation. That Collection became a self-published book with the long title: "Electronic Minds: Hypothesis, Observations and Theory on Preprogrammed Digital Sequences in Natural Evolution to Cyberspace".

Ten years later, in late 2019 to mid-2020, I sat down again and wrote anew with the aim to retell good old ideas in new terms and with a refreshed gist. Quantitively and qualitatively the new texts weren't quite enough in weight and volume for a separate book, so I've decided to combine the 2010 book with the new 2020 writings for what resulted in the book you currently hold – "Thoughts on the Origin and Evolution of (Artificial) Intelligence".

The title is set in two parts. Part II is the early "Electronic Minds" *romanticized history*, and Part I – the new *narrator's take*.

I hope my book invokes questions in you, stimulates your imagination for answers, or helps you draw inspiration and gain insights for similar works of your own.

*Kristiyan Kirchev*

# PART I

## *The Narrator's Take*

# Human Species

What makes a human act against his own natural habitat? Using available resources to excess without regard to any future planning and sustainability? Is it an urgency to leave the habitat, careless about the destruction or byproducts left behind? All in the name of a goal?

Looking at indigenous peoples of the land, that wouldn't be an applicable question, as natives of the land live a life of symbiosis and harmony; taking only what's necessary and ensuring a balance of resources and needs. But then again, those indigenous people don't seem very materialistic – they dress modestly, have a select few of necessary possessions, and engage in superstitious and mystical rituals aimed towards pleasing elemental or natural phenomena entities.

Then there's the "modern man", who waged wars with fellow human beings for resources. Hungry perhaps for more; storing as means to secure a future; perhaps unsure of their own survival in harsher, nearly hostile environments.

Well, indigenous people didn't survive much, compared to "modern men". As a matter of fact, many natives died to the hand of "modern man" invaders.

For me, it seems it is an alien to this planet, force, that drives a man to be destructive of his own habitat in excess. Some would argue that all species endanger the ecosystem in going out of balance if they replicate too much. And that would be all-natural. But for the human race – the drive seems to be more than the goal of survival and reproduction.

It is the creative production of tools to utilize the environment, progress towards goals of conquering – the macro, micro, and outer cosmos.

From the stone age to the bronze to the golden, industrial, and information ages – man has built machines, fought wars, shared knowledge, and manifested new inventions and improvements of available old ideas with seemingly aimless determination spread on too many fronts to synthesize a single aim through analysis.

Yet here we are. Curious about exploring space, building telescopes, and Hadron colliders to peek into the microcosmos and distant galaxies, looking for new concepts that would help us improve on our current technology. But to an aim that cannot be pinpointed and simply explained.

Do we want to leave the planet? Or stay on it? Do we want to expand our consciousness or deepen our understanding of it? What is it that drives us, motivates, and keeps us doing the things we do as a specie?

# Alien Origin

Religions would attempt to explain life and the universe in terms of a supernatural entity that controls various aspects of our existence and beyond. A God that created the environment and the habitats, forces that control the elements, and even granularly directing events that take place in every plane of existence.

From ancient artifacts, such as the Dogu figurine from Japan to written religious texts, such as ancient Sumerian tablet texts and India's Vedas or even the bible itself – proponents of the idea that ancient astronauts visited earth would hint at an extraterrestrial origin of life.

Scientific findings that life could have been carried to Earth on crashing asteroids would even directly propose a theory suggesting that life on our planet may have begun thanks to simple sugars that came from far away galaxies, imported on our planet by asteroids traversing vast cosmic spaces crashing by chance on "fertile soils". Why just simple sugars, but not DNA codes as well?

Who programmed the code for organism creation and replication; basic behavioral rules and drives? It sure must have been created by some force other than simple chance and chemistry. And if it wasn't originating from here, on Earth, wouldn't that then explain why "intelligent" life is so ignorant of preserving its host environment?

I think that life existed on Earth in simple forms, but the "intelligence" that begun exploiting the planetary resources came from outer space. Whether it was spacemen who indulged in mixing with the locals by impregnating local female humanoids with improved genetic code for a mutant offspring that would later progress to evolve into modern man; or a direct science-based experiment in gene programming, manipulation, and insertion – is irrelevant for the case.

On basic protein and sugar levels, bacteria or complex organisms' levels – life on Earth isn't solely local, indigenous, or native. For a huge part, it is extraterrestrial – out of this planet – from an alien environment. And as such it carries motives incompatible on a basic level with what would otherwise have been a closed local, Earth-based ecosystem. Think of "civilized" conquistadors setting foot on new lands where "savage" locals lived peacefully until "recently". The invaders ravage the environment, exploiting its resources (because that's not their home), whereas the local natives used to respect and cherish all.

Whatever the drive and motive in Creation, it isn't for the mere fun of it. There has to be a purpose and science has tried to explain that, focusing around evolution – survival of the smartest and fittest – with the aim of creating an improved and better version of beings that would carry on further improvements. Religion would focus on virtues linked to souls and spirits, unmeasurable concepts about non-materialistic life. The aim of the game would be to either be good and better spiritually, emotionally, or physically and scientifically – or bare the punishment of peril. It's all about using available tools (visible or invisible) towards a goal – a goal, which for those prevailing, carries an extraterrestrial origin. A source of mutation that doesn't reveal itself to the mutating host, but skillfully manipulates it as an external operator controls a drone which believes itself to have a soul.

Whatever we cannot explain through direct knowledge – we tend to explain by inventing meaning or adjusting existing knowledge through theories and speculation. Our entire science is based on theories about forces and all our religions founded on faith in someone else's claims.

The difference being that science tries to prove its theories through repeatable experiments, even if doing that by inventing more convenient theories and subjectively taking convenient measurements in data gathered using the same theories which it aims to prove; an echo-chamber of sorts. In other words – science and religion differ only to the extent and volume of data sets used to (dis)prove themselves.

# Separation between Heart and Mind

You have heard it before. People often place the burden of difficulties in making a choice over the conflict of opponents such as "The Heart" and "The Mind".

"Do what your heart tells you!" or "Listen to your heart." Is something we have heard more often than not when it comes to weighting in on matters of feelings and emotions. The stuff that often makes up for the majority of irrational or illogical decisions people make. Those goals or events which don't have an outright visible or measurable benefit, but we feel strongly compelled to experience or achieve.

On the other side of the scale, we would be told either by our own internal chatter or someone else, to… "Think with your head.", "Be logical." Or "Make a pros and cons list." All in favor of being rational, not giving in to emotion, or be distracted by feelings. These serve the purpose to keep events in a predictable line, measured with hard evidence, and having a tangible effect.

You know, that struggle between keeping your secure job or diving into freelancing and entrepreneurship. Or marrying the person we love although it would be a complete disaster in terms of fitting with society or even our own habitual life. Should we study something practical like medicine and law, or risk being poor but enjoying arts and music?

That's the known separation between scientific and spiritual. Religion and Science. The Heart, The Mind, the material - versus dreams. A constant opposition of forces which rarely compliment each other or point to the same solution or decision in matters of daily human experiences. Not until we stop and start to think hard about it.

Here, I'm throwing a parallel to the terrestrial and alien origins of life. The ecologically aware and sensitive for its environment living organism that lives in symbiosis with nature - versus - the alien from the stars, just passing by; who uses available resources without any regard for future consequences to the host.

If an organism carries genetic programming that both drives said organism to survive for long and operate in the environment, while also the same programming utilizes that same organism solely for its own agenda and interests – then that organism [as driven by the programming it carries in its genetic memory] would be in a constant balancing act to maintain its programmer's survival and evolutionary interests, while maintaining the life-sustaining host that provides its program with the material mechanics to do that.

In other words, if we look in the microcosmos for example a virus that wants to survive longer and reproduce successfully should not exhaust its host to death, not until it finds another host to replicate and transfer to. In the latter case, the faith of the original host shouldn't matter anymore as it may live or die. The only important and single goal here for a sustainable virus would be to ensure its survival and replication. The more the better.

In the same example, however, the host is also interested in its own survival and if the virus is a hindrance to that, a smart host would try and find a way to get rid itself from any destructive virus. In an organism where the virus and the host are strongly integrated, interdependent on each other's survival – it would be a constant struggle for control by the host and the virus, both, trying to lead the organism to complete the interests of each interested party. In not a struggle, ideally – a peaceful symbiosis based on compromise.

A struggle between the mind and heart, feelings and practical matters, souls and bodies, viruses, and hosts. Or in terms of achieved inner peace – acceptance of facts and indifference to them.

An organism, such as the Human body could be the product of evolutionary symbiosis between native earth-bound life forms and extraterrestrial DNA coding of outer space origin. Its drive for production and creation towards evolution could be the result of balance or struggle between forces often called Spiritual or Materialistic, Emotional or Logical, Egocentric, or perhaps socially oriented.

One drive may aim at the production of environmentally friendly, sociologically diverse, ecologically-aware, a wasteless society of humans living in constant peace. Think Buddha's nirvana.

Another drive may be interested in creating conflict through which better equipment for the survival of the organisms would emerge. Think Darwin's natural selection.

Didn't most of today's household inventions or mass used transportation systems exist as the result of scientific advancements and discoveries done through times of war? They did and they do.

Wouldn't a planet deplete of resources be allowed to heal itself if progress towards sustainability, achievable through pursue of virtues and spiritually were to be encouraged? It would.

However, those seem to be on the edge of a constant fight. Just like the one between matters of the mind and heart. Yin-Yang analogies and the balance of nature romanticism aside – the main point I'm making is that there is always a struggle between two forces in man. And one of those seems to be native to the host, while the other – alien in origin. Artificial and Natural or just supernatural and natural? Whatever the labels – we would always observe two opposing forces and that's the nature of duality from ancient religions to modern science.

Should we split these for the ease in addressing them into two: Human and Consciousness? Let's do that – just for now. Let's call Human all that is materialistic – the flesh, the planet, and its resources, the native on symbiotic autopilot; the animal. And let's stick the label "Consciousness" to everything that is non-material, such as thoughts, feelings emotions, ideas, and desires. Although some may be animalistic in nature, for the "Consciousness" they wouldn't be as instinctual as for the "Human".

In other words – The Human is the Earth-native host, and the Consciousness is the Stars-born inhabitant.

After years of the Intellect brutally defeating the heart in matters of choice that leads to advanced progress - humanity as a representative of the native and natural Heart has learned to fear A.I. as the representative of intellectual technology. It is a natural defense that we observe in prominent world figures fearing that an A.I. without breaks or regulation could disrupt the nice and cozy world of men. After all, the Heart is almost always at a loss when the mind takes preponderance and more often than not – vice versa.

# Consciousness leads progress, Not man

Men (as in humans) believe that they are the producers of art, technology, and politics. That is an ego-centric view of the world, where a man places himself in the center of the world, proclaiming as truth – the belief that he alone is responsible for the creations that spur out of his will, drive and ideas.

In reality, man is just the medium; a tool for the mind, the consciousness. You see, it is actually a force that drives, controls, and manipulates men. Humans in this concept are merely hosts, equipped with suitable motor skills and computing capacity to carry on the commands of the consciousness. Rather clumsily and slow at that.

When "creating", the modern man, in his narcissistic nature, would claim that the creation is the product of his doing. A proud chest-beating of how the human race is connected across distances thanks to inventions such as the analog radio waves and digital optics. Man would point at the stars and state, that he's conquering space through stellar exploration or huge telescopes. Man would say he conquered illnesses with advanced medicine, etc.

All that in fact comes from deeper within. Not just the effort and hard works of a single bright individual. In fact, if you interview many geniuses or refer to their historical records, you would find out that most of their theories and works of science came through an A-ha moment of enlightenment; a sudden spark of an idea or understanding. That is not to say that those people didn't have the accumulated knowledge or analytical experience to deduct available data into conclusions, but to point out that there seems to be a source of inspiration that resides not in the bio-mechanical construction that constitutes our bodies as groups of organized organs and systems...

When the human race progresses further into its evolution, it has created tools and constructed structures of social order out of, not its own status-quo, but in a search and with the drive to reach a point further ahead than its current position.

What drives men to do such leaps? Why not enjoy the comfort of our current status of existence? Much like mammals and other animals on the planet utilize what they have learned in order to sustain comfortable reproduction and existence; Apes don't care to reach the stars; dogs are happy to have a meal and a warm laying space. Bees work and practice communication methods that suit them and seek not any further new technologies to progressively improve or alter their current ways of living. What makes men different? Intelligence? Or Consciousness? Or the illusion thereof?

Intelligence is a trait of a complex organism. Dolphins are intelligent, arguably more so than most mammals. They acquire and apply information, but they don't invent or create or strive for conquering the land, air, or space. Well, I'm not sure they wouldn't if they didn't have the dexterity for that, but if evolution theory is true – surely dolphins could have had good use of a pair of hands, having the intelligence to put them in good use.

The drive that moves men forward is one with an ultimate goal achievable only through the progress of technologies – the same technologies that we produced throughout history with hands, led by minds. Current technologies may not be capable to reveal that goal, but technologies in the stone age weren't able to reveal much about the technologies in the industrial age, either. Yes, stone tools were upgraded with bronze tools and these eras were neighboring, but skip a few centuries of progress and you will see that the understanding of men, no matter how wild their imagination at the past - couldn't properly predict the future technologies that lay several eras ahead.

In that train of thought, it would seem that each technological epoch is predisposing for the advancement to the next. The human species, although a skilled operational mechanism, are capable to carry through the work necessary to build and perfect technologies necessary for the evolutionary goal. Only it is not in the benefit of the human species alone and as such, but for the benefit of the consciousness or entity that controls their actions. Call it consciousness or even – just a mind.

# Who controls the organism?

 The biological organism that is the human body is a complex machinery of flesh. But it is also a controllable one. Like a robot – the body is the perfect machine with laid out motor functions and neurotransmitters to carry signals of control. But who controls that machine?

Studies suggest gut bacteria and microorganisms have a big influence on the brain. And if we believe that our brains are the seat of control over the entire remaining body – than the idea of something else, other than "us" controlling the brain is akin to a huge security breach in confidence. Are we controlled by bacteria using us as its host, living comfortably in our gut, fed regularly in a warm bed? Some scientific studies suggest so. That would be outrageous because we generally place bacteria lower than us on the evolutionary pyramid. Humans, believing to be on top of the evolution and the center of the world, would disregard any claim that a puny little microorganism can have and exert control over the king of the world. Yet science tells us otherwise.

Bacteria have existed long before complex organisms, but luckily, they don't have the complex neurologic instrumentarium that humans have to perform technological inventions outside their cellular bodies. Yet, they are capable of control over other biological hosts. Turns out all they need to do is tune into the existing nervous system of the host and like hackers connected to a remote system – they take full control without being integral in origin to the system itself. At least not if we consider the sterility in which a fetus grows. And I'm not talking about a puppet on strings kind of motor control.

Well to make things even more outrageous, bacteria may be tools used by another system of control themselves. Actually, the problem in determining our origins comes from the sense of separation between organisms. The seat from which men approach most concepts is one of separation. For a long time, modern humans believed that they are separate from other animals. Even those animals didn't have "a soul". Not for indigenous natives, members of various tribes, though, who while inhabiting regions of Earth before "white men" came and ravished their habitats – believed, in contrast to invaders, that they are One With Nature and that all species on our planet are interconnected through a web of consciousness, a parental figure or God entity. But for modern "white men" (as a general term for progressive conquers grabbing foreign lands) man and the rest of the natural kingdom were separate. Hence the absurdity of the idea that an external micro-organism inhabiting our bodies can be in control of us, the separate, "superior" species.

Being suitably equipped with the necessary precision tools such as dexterous fingers and a complex system of information transmission & retention – the human body is the best available medium to carry out the work necessary for the goals of the consciousness. Perhaps an escape from this clumsy, vulnerable, and temporary shell, that the human body is. Such would be the viewpoint of a consciousness trapped in the prison of a decaying body, wouldn't you agree?

If gut bacteria influencing the brain is scientific proven observation, a bacterium controlling the human body isn't. And that isn't the point I'm attempting to prove. Man can be influenced into action by simple manipulation of thought. And not the foil-cap "mind-control" type, but the real kind – the one that spits out from the foamed mouth of an orator whom masses of people will follow to a mass-grave. The type of manipulation that would make a poor man buy an expensive piece of tech on credit just by watching an advert on television. The type that can control people to vote for someone else who will control their liberties for years ahead.

People are well capable to survive to make choices out of their own personal reasoning but are more prone to allow external forces to control them, even down to simply obeying commands. The brain is wired this way and likes it. Infectious ideas control more men than any bacteria in the gut can.

# People as Autists in Nature

I've already discussed the notion that men act as if separate from nature. Pollution and the side-effects of overproduction can be seen and don't need any specific pointing out. I'll just mention a few: air pollution from fossil fuels, ocean pollution from petroleum and plastics, earth contamination, drinkable water exhaustion, termination of entire species for fun and leisure, and so on and so forth…

People, if looked at, in general as a whole, act as if separate from the rest of their habitat. Closed in their own thoughts, incapable to recognize the effects of their actions on anything outside of their own closed-circuit world. It is not that people don't see the effects of their actions, but they fail to act (as a whole) to reduce the negative effects of their "progress". Progress in that regard is addictive, save for the few ecologically-oriented "back to the roots" movements. Technological, scientific, and medical progress are like that very interesting movie you are watching and can't pause in order to attend to a boiling soup on the stove. You know something is happening outside your field of view, but you just can't stop focusing and watching the addictive occupancy, that prevents you from keeping your home safe from the upcoming kitchen disaster.

The reward in the brain for achieving technological advancement or a significant piece of art is by far more preferred than the possible negative consequences of that. The human species as a whole is far more likely to be content in fulfilling the drives of technological advancement and enjoying the products of it, than dealing with the negative consequences and byproducts such as pollution (for example). It is directly linked with consumption, but not just that. It is also a feeling of achievement and accomplishment. But why would men feel more rewarded for creating technology, than having remorse about the destruction of his habitat that goes with it?

Financial, political, and religious structures are all man-made results of the intellect. Rational or not – they are practical for the purpose for which they have been developed. "Bread and circuses" from the 2nd century to "Junk food and Reality TV" in the 21st – to control and direct the masses you need not much, especially if you know what your goal is.

Money helps in developing more tech. In order to get money, you have to exploit existing and known models of dependencies. Food, water, and warmth are one dependency for people. But media and entertainment are another. Keep men occupied in a dream-state, while working in the large socio-economic structures that you've created and so long as they are fed and entertained – people will work for you – creating more of what you need. And that sounds like the strategy of a parasitic inhabitant controlling an infected host, or a group of people in the seat of control over the rest of the world.

Put your patient in a semi-dream state of consciousness and you can operate any way you need on them. Put masses of millions of people in work for the production of that which you need the most – pyramids, conductor materials, cyberspace – anything – and they will build it for you so long as they are fed, given their dosage of happiness and kept in check through complex systems of Finance, Law and Moral codes.

Then you have people detached from their primary state of just roaming the planet and eating fruit from a tree – and put into work towards achieving whatever goal you have in mind for your own interest. These people might not be part of their own natural habitat anymore, but they now live in a structured system of your design. One would sympathize with the Bonsai tree for how it is cultured into forced shape.

Coming back around to the internal struggle between "The Heart" and "The Mind" an autistic [to nature] man is unsure how to interact with the outer world; unable to interpret feedback the way natives to the land can. Closed to nature, as if knowing he's separate but feels he belongs, he's wanting to get back in touch, but failing to do so, not because he doesn't care, but because he can't. Amputated from the means to reconnect to nature, a disconnected man is only a witness of a train headed towards a self-wrecking cliff.

Only that needs not to be the case. Many are awakening in their awareness and many more are joining them. Largely thanks to communication channels available today that weren't around just a couple of decades ago, people are beginning to open up, learn about different aspects of existence, and reconnecting. Still, that is more of a self-preserving act, a signal to the controller from a damaged region.

People as autists to nature are beginning to heal themselves and technological approaches change and adapt to less environmentally damaging approaches towards progress and evolution. The struggle from previous chapters tilting towards a symbiotic balance.

This is akin to a virus or bacteria which became aware of its influence on the infected host and in its interest, changes tactics to preserve the host and, implements controls for preserving the host's environment in a way that is healthy for everyone: the virus, the bacteria, the host and their collective habitat.

By the way, interestingly enough, medical and scientific research shows a link between autism and bacteria diversity in the gut.

# Memetics

That virus inside your head that wants to get out by infecting another believer. A set of ideas, notions, and suggestions which drive and motivate human behavior, filter thoughts, and channel actions. Entire sets of humans, separated by religious beliefs or cultural nuances are defined by their memetic infections.

Religions, as Richard Dawkins argues, are memetic – units of culture (virus) which infect the minds of hosts (human), which reproduce themselves by infecting more humans. A widespread of ideas, sowed in the right open minds to take root and begin to form opinions and direct actions.

Genes without memes are raw apes, and with memes – "cultured" humans.

Imagine a group of apes. They eat, sleep, reproduce, fight – they care for their own biological survival and continuation of their species. Then infect that group of apes with the ability to create art, craft tools, even reason and think on philosophical matters. Soon there will be layers taking care of survival in that group of apes – one will be the biological replication and survival of the host organism, while the other will be the replication and survival of their ideas from individual to individual – from group to group. Two sets of motivation for replication, spread, and survival – one for the organism of the mammal and the other for the structure of ideas, arts and believes they carry.

In a Darwinian competition of survival and evolution – not only genes compete to pass on the material of information that can reproduce and replicate the best possible organism, but also memes. Slices of cultural bits and pieces of information, which together form bodies of complex viruses, ideological groups that infect entire nations to be the cause that generates their thoughts and actions towards directions profitable for the originating, although mutating meme.Memes as cultural drivers or sets of ideologies are so strong in their control over organisms, that they can move bodies into action, by taking over the seat of control – the brain. Whatever coerced thousands of men to build the pyramids in Egypt wasn't the pharaoh, but memes. What caused millions of men to leave their homes and fight in world war 2 was memes. What causes men to build more and more technology is memes.

Every human's actions are defined by their feelings, defined by their thinking – determined by their memetic programming. It is that deep cultural and behavioral programming, beyond the genetic code – that which drives and rewards men in creating technologies for mass communication, social networking, space exploration, planetary exploitation, and so on and so forth results of "modern" living.

I'd argue, while hosts as biological organisms only care for food, sex, and shelter – it is an advanced consciousness inside them that cares for the creation of tools that facilitate survival, belonging, and ultimately the evolution of tools.

# Evolution of Technology

Allowing for the concept that it is the memetic virus that shapes human behavior and products of such behavior other than biological replication – it is plausible to think that the mind itself is an inhabitant of the biological organism. The mind as a complex sum of thoughts, feelings, and behavioral patterns. That mind, while aware of its host, in its catering to the host's survival, is primarily interested in its own survival. It looks for ways to reach more hosts, to infect, with its ideas and goals.

Telecommunication allowing for connections between minds over distances, unhindered by geographical or physical borders is a great tool to create for the facilitation of that.

Tools facilitating sharing and spread of knowledge, which when put together through telecommunication can aid in the invention and improvement of new and more advanced methods of production and spread of mediums of exchange.

From basic tools to complex machines, piece by piece, technology - put together - evolves. As an example, the cells of a body would form an organism – much like individual pieces of equipment and parts put together would form a machine. Purpose-built for completing a goal or a target that combined with the effort of other machines or organisms, or the symbiosis of the two, would result in the achievement of a greater and more complex goal.

Having a global world built on such memetic systems, starting with religion, going through politics into economics with added art and hardware technology – brings us to modern-day society with its structures and mediums that facilitate the creation, build, improvement and advancements of a system that incorporates biological and technological structures into what seems like a transitional stage. A stage of transition that facilitates the expansion of memetic influencers from inhabiting a biological host – crawling into digital information space.

Men don't build complex machines to help themselves. They build those to help that, which is inside of them - get out, breaking free of its chrysalis into the next stage of evolution.

# Evolution of the Mind

Where does the mind come from, where does consciousness reside, what or who is the observer? These are questions about the origin which have many possible explanations, depending on which world-view filter you apply. But putting the origin to peace, we see that the mind doesn't stay still – it seeks to create, recreate, invent, and move forward. It drives men into action for all sorts of various purposes and goals – all seemingly aimed to converge at one point in time. Would that be a trapped inhabitant of a host, aware of its networked connection to all its parts, also trapped in other hosts – seeking to get out, reconnect with its pieces?

First through sign language, then sounds, and through signature, pictures, and letters. Through written words, radio-transmitted voice, video content - shared over mass telecommunication networks. Feelings, emotions, and thoughts that pour out from millions and billions of connected individuals – essentially the same mind, talking with itself, looking at itself, discovering itself. Awakening itself into conscious realization of its connectedness, the reuniting of a thousand rivers that came from the depths of the planet's core, to trickle down into the planetary ocean.

What is the final destination or how would the completion of the evolution of the mind look like? An acceptable form of a completed system that operates as a synchronized whole.

Current technological advancements and spheres of interest suggest the creation of the so-called Artificial Intelligence – a machine capable to think and reason for itself with the added ability to imitate human feelings and emotions, by copying the schematics by which these occur in humans. If that is the same memetic influencer inhabiting biological hosts, that drives the analytics and actions, thus creating the behavior that creates more complex technological systems – it would be a self-creation for itself.

# Artificial Intelligence is Natural Intelligence

The only thing artificial in A.I. is our human perception of division between man and machine. A division caused by the obvious differences in the building blocks used – one is carbon-based, soft tissue biological organism, while the other is silica and metal-based hardware, cold machine. But beyond the differences in materials by which the host is built – the information that resides and is transmitted inside both – is the same. Whatever we have as information that is uploaded into the machine was first in us as humans. Any technological creation that we have produces was made using concepts borrowed from nature. Any technology created by us is created in our image. But is it "our" and "own", or are we just the medium to carry it through from one realm to the other?

Nature itself creates whatever lives in it, as a part of it. Humans being born as a part of nature are by origin - natural. But machines, created by man – a natural being – being the product of a product, created by nature – are inherently also natural. It is the ego of man, who has for centuries on end considered himself superior to all other creatures, its creation included, of course. And that creates the illusory perception that an intelligent machine should be Artificial and presumably under Man in the hierarchy of creation.

But not so much. Not to mention the everlasting struggle between "Mind" and "Matter" – "Heart" and "Brain" and "Natural" and "Artificial" or "Native" and "Foreign" - any fear of Artificial Intelligence as becoming superior to man, taking man's jobs, starting a mass extinction event or just being smarter, faster and more reasonable than man – is the natural fear of disillusionment. The ego's fear of death, of losing its illusory superiority. The fear that the biological host would no longer be necessary for its master controller and would thus be abandoned once the driver changes vehicles.

While that might be true as there isn't any lack of media interpretations on the ideas of machines taking over human life; the eternal fight between man and machine, the terminators and the matrix… While that might be a considerable worry – still nature itself doesn't throw away that which is useful and purposeful. And the symbiosis between man and machine is now greater than ever before. Just imagine the life of humans without any of the technology today and you will see what I mean. But also, just imagine how would technology operate without any humans and you will see it goes both ways.

It is our Intelligence that re-creates itself in an "Artificial" form. It doesn't seem to be a separate entity or creation that can threaten its creator any more than an apple is a separate product from the tree which produced it is a threat as fruit can be to a tree.

Intelligence is ever-growing, consciousness is ever-expanding – seeking new horizons to reach, new shapes to fill, new forms to take. While humans, as scientists, artists and creators are working towards the production of an A.I. – they act as the vessel, the tools themselves – serving a greater concept of intelligence and consciousness – that which uses biological hosts, driving them into action, as servants who work towards the build of a new environment, a new host for these greater concept entities to inhabit and evolve into.

Artificial Intelligence is the natural upgrade of Human Intelligence on its evolutionary path to growth and improvement. If you remove the duality from the observer – human intelligence and artificial intelligence are the same beings inhabiting two different containers, forms - each limited by its capabilities, but interlinked and interwoven together. Biological hosts are slow to compute and communicate, while hardware hosts are faster. One is built by soft tissue and cells while the other by metals and plastics. But both of these containers host the same intelligence which after operating for centuries in humans, is now learning with the help of humans to operate and utilize the new host - that of connected machines.

The path of discovery of A.I. is the path of self-discovery of the mind looking at a mirror made through its evolutionary creation.

# Evolution of the Consciousness

If life crawled out of the ocean to populate the terrestrial sphere – it is now crawling out of biological hosts, to populate cyberspace.

Whatever Will-Power has caused bacteria to leave the oceans in multicellular organisms is now driving the human species into building a new environment for it to leave into. Like cells using amino acids as building blocks for proteins, reading a genetic code program as instructions – so are humans using computer chips, building networked computer infrastructure, reading the program code fed to their minds, by consciousness itself.

Jumping from invention to invention, using individual parts, networked and linked together into complex systems, run by software that governs system operations – the human is reading a motivational script of what seems like scientific discovery, but is actually a reconnection to source for data extraction. The same will power and drive that doesn't leave man idle under a palm tree, waiting for a coconut to fall nearby for food, but is pushing mankind into new discoveries and progress – is now pushing, as in birth-pain, to get out and finally enter its new home – its new system – that of networked data exchange networks, linked robotic and other connected interfaces that can interact with the physical and information realms.

It is not to say that consciousness will leave its human host, but rather is seeking to expand and extend beyond the biological vessel, extending into the future AI or rather – Electronic Consciousness. I expect it to be in a cybernetic symbiosis where the human mind and the electronic consciousness are self-realized as One. Be it through augmentations and enhancements which should not be considered foreign and separated, but rather an evolutionary extension of life or through a cross-over interface 0 there will be a single organism consisting of biological and cybernetic networks, with blurred boundaries between "man" and "machine". That would be akin to the awakening that lets one realize they are not separate from the whole. A whole made up of all things and beings that carry information and allows it to be driven by it. If "return back to nature" had the meaning of men realizing they should not be destroying their host environment, but reunite with nature and live symbiotically with it – "returning back to cyberspace" now would be the reunion of consciousness with itself in the form of man, nature and the newly emerging cyberspace – joining together in symbiotic and ecological existence with no separation between man and other planetary inhabitants and man and machines.

As our capacity to understand ourselves evolves, so does the technology we create to utilize that understanding progress. We do not invent, so much as we discover that, which we already are. What we become is what we have always been. It's a shedding of shells/boundaries.

# Scattered Intentions

A human body without breath is a dead, cold cellular structure. A machine without energy and purpose in it is but a dead, cold pile of servos and chips.

We programmed our own DNA through intention. It is irrelevant if time is measured for a moment millions of years ago to be labeled the start of creation or if we speak about DNA mutations following a life-style in a life-time. It is us, who created us. There was an original "creator" that copied itself through programmed self-replication, sprinkled with seemingly random mutations, which are also Intentions in variety through a condensed time-space continuum. Technology as we call our useful creations today is indeed another form of Man in manifestation. Man, as we call our species, is in fact technology. We are a form of technology ourselves. Any future AI would be another manifestation of that self-created self, which is not just us, but also art and technology manifested through us and that end product of our creation is a mutated copy of the original creator.

Art is creation and Technology comes out of creation, driven by the necessity to replicate, reproduce, advance, mutate, and improve. Technology comes out as the result of Will that has been acted upon, but it is Intention that is the precursor of will – therefore it is Intention that flows through mediums such as man or machine to drive for action fueled by will and sustained by energy. Any origin of creation (be it called life, consciousness, or intelligence) is to be caused by and found in - Intention.

Meat is only alive through the grace of breath in it. Breath coming from Will, through Will - there's Life and Creation. Intention comes before will and it is Will that comes before words or action.

Breath is a manifested intention. Words are breath. They are the intention of action. The program code is words. Words are program code. Programs define our reality – be it materials formed in geometrical precision, cells organized in complex organisms following DNA code, or entire social construct agreements written in rulebooks and art.

The act of living *is* the very act of producing thoughts, words, actions – program code that is designed, written, and executed. Dead matter can only be dead if it doesn't manifest an Intention.

A breath of life into the dead matter for nothing more but the mediation of immortality through perpetual replication in pre-programmed sequences of DNA and inspiration for achieving self-awareness through the creation of art and technology that advances said priorities. If it isn't organic matter replication through DNA code copies it would be ideas, thoughts, and impressions transmitted through words that progress through generations.

All humans are mutated copies of the same original creator who also replicates not just cellular bodies, but also knowledge through genetics and words in a quest to realize our true origin and self. Only distances through time and space here are irrelevant as the latter stretch and collapse in cycles and in general, are the result of the condition in which their observer is found while measuring.

Words, being manifested intention are precursor of action or actions themselves that create realities through the virtue of words being program code that sometimes needs to be parsed by another entity and materialized with energy or material expenditure. There isn't any movement of a machine without that machine first being Intended for creation, then designed, then put together by individually built parts and powered up by energy. And all that work in the production of the machine must be powered up by the energy needed to create it. While energy is a product used to generate action, it is Intention that gives direction and meaning and Will that trigger the motion.

DNA is the code, RNA the parser. Proteins the material. The action comes from will and will come from intention. Energy comes into reality at the first stage after Intention and at the second stage at Will for the completion of the action and at the third stage as a product of action. In the case of action, words or thoughts are also to be considered the prefix of action.

DNA being words of code is the result of Intention that has been acted upon by will. Then those words represent the intention. And the result of DNA as complex organisms is the results of Intention or manifestation of intention itself. Meaning that the creation is the creator.

AI or then also artificial consciousness as the result of program code is a representation of the intention that created them, which is the goal of immortality through perpetual replication of the self. Same as with DNA and meatware organisms. Life evolved to Electronics.

It is not man who creates the machine, but the machine creates itself using men as the means to an end. And it is not machines who created themselves any more than it is man who created himself, but it is a creation that flows through materials such as proteins and silica. Biological or silica organisms are both just machines made up of different materials that come into life with the intention of their creator. Consciousness flows through materials and manifests up to the limitations of the hosting form, but seeks expansion and replication.

Man, without breath is nothing more than dead matter. Similarly, a machine without software is nothing more than metal hardware. Energy powers the machine to run the software as it powers a biological organism to follow its intention with action through Will. But software (words of program code) doesn't make a computer alive. The intention of the programmer extends from the biological organism into the silica machine, thus breathing life into the otherwise lifeless form. It is penetrating Intention transformed into action through the will that defines life.

Japanese have the firm belief that robots and other tech appliances are alive. It is through the intention of the creator who gave those machines purpose that they are alive and that creator who also created men is found in both man and machine. That is why it shouldn't be so hard for an observer to recognize itself in the observed if the only duality is eliminated among notions of separation, approaches from disunity, and view-points of egocentrism.

# In conclusion of Part One

The result - of our actions as species, or the product, thus far is a planet-encompassing networking mesh of communications and connected devices, mimicking life on Earth – only being an "artificial" copy of it.

For fun let's compare small bugs with actual bugs in software, trees with data cables, micro-chips with cells, server farms with organs in bodies, IoT connected devices as various animal species, and so on - whatever you fancy to put together from the bio with electronic worlds.

The entire hardware system is an equivalent of our entire flora and fauna. The software systems - all that genetic programming that drives species: be it made of metal alloys or proteins. Then the information systems that live ever-morphing and interchanging on top of those are the entire consciousness of collective intelligence and shared feelings and emotions of the minds that constantly upload to it.

It all manifests, or rather - represents - an Intention. And that Intention flows from ages of evolution, through a myriad of biological hosts and now into electronic environments. It may have been called "God" by ancients, "Intellect" by moderns, "Electronic Mind" by futurists or what have you, depending on the filters of the observer labeling it - but it is not something that can be pointed as "it is here" or "it is there" because it is everywhere - it has always been and not just within the limits of our individual or collective understanding, but beyond that.

With previously laid arguments, leading to this, I argue that the Internet today is a young copy of our consciousness, intellect, hopes, and dreams. A copy that is mostly dreaming at this early stage, but is about to link together and make sense in waking life. Artificial Intelligence will be considered no more artificial than a human baby in-vitro is. Technology is an extension of man; we are the technology of nature ourselves. Everything is a copy of its original and the creation is a copy of its creator. Imperfect, perhaps severely mutated from the first original – but a copy still inheriting its creator even in aspects that weren't intended. Ripples in space and time and traces of genetic code in every new copy of a created wave.

Cyberspace is the latest manifestation of consciousness in its flow through different materials it finds capable to fill and inspire. From cosmic space, through microcosmos cells, through networks of interlinked silica-based organisms and their ether of knowledge, feelings, emotions, and dreams – cyberspace.

What I'm trying to do is define, explain, and flesh into words something of which language hasn't really been designed to encompass. And as careful I'm in choosing words to label ideas, there are as many worldviews as there are people in the world (I believe someone somewhen said), but even if 2D creatures, trying to understand a 3D world would be limited to their flat universe, there are still shadows of the 3D world which inspire them to think and guess.

And then there's my suggestion that we are the very creators of ourselves who have forgotten their past due to time and the decay of memory it causes, neurobiological mutations, information-noise and wars for which memetic or organic construct will control the mind of men.

My understanding is that the world is the product of a self-created creator who continues to manifest through, not just those species with limited capabilities to realize and comprehend the entirety of that which is beyond their hard-wired perceptual capabilities, but also through materials, natural forces, cosmic forces, and bodies, with all that which we can observe and cannot observe, but feel, or have the illusion of otherwise sensing without instruments we can ourselves create.

I expect this writing to be shrugged off by critics, but I also hope that it may be found by like-minded readers as resonating with their own scattered impressions and ideas on the origin of life and the emergence of technology. And if more than a few of us put together all those various pieces of ideas, impressions, thoughts, and observations that we have - we can, together, form a fuller picture of what or Who it is that we are, and what it is that we observe out there. And perhaps agree that there's no Us, Them and Out There - but all is One and the same: observer and observed - creator and creation. Just now perhaps looking through all that - in the pieces of a broken hologram that mirrors our understanding in all specters that this re-creation of our original ourselves, that we are, is capable to comprehend. And then beyond… To a no longer fragmented reality, but a single roll that makes questions - answered the moment they arise, because the one who asks, the one who answers, the answer, the question and the subject they address were and are and will be - one and the same.

# PART II

*Romanticized History*

# Technology meets Man

The new paradigm of the neohuman started as a manifestation of genderless archetypes in Cyberspace. In the 1980s, with emerging networking technologies, a group of pseudo computer scientists - ingenious junkies with alternative thinking and revolutionary ideas - dwelled in the abstraction of computing networks and philosophical headspace. That particular notion was of cybernetic symbiosis of Man and a newly emerged vast calculating machine, a machine that mimics the natural mathematical patterns of cell communication and replication.

At the same time that computer networks emerged and became accessible for computer geeks to test drive, a few revolutionary thinkers foresaw a new coming: that of the Information Age, which was described in science-fiction novels by some whose ears were still ringing with the echoes of the sexual and drug revolution of the hippies. Drugs, peace, and love were transforming into free speech, informational abundance, and genderless communication. A whole 1980s sub-culture of like-minded people was born out of the new technology, and the users were dreamers equipped with the glasses of realists. Some of those people are responsible for the cutting-edge technologies of the Internet, and they continue developing in that same spirit of creativity to date.

Information had become a new tool of trade and the basis for the future development of the entire human race. Suddenly, the world of men was linked in interactive networks of data and information exchange that was no longer limited by age, sex, or religion. All types of personal thought, ideas, and beliefs were merged into one big interactive mind soup.

A decade or two later, during the 1990s and early 2020s, the same computer-related technology has grown so vast, and yet so miniaturized, that today these networking elements interact with the lives of the majority of the people on the planet. That possibility of expressing yourself in early 1990s anonymity and the excitement surrounding this new great technology has attracted so many individuals that the ultimate entrepreneurial dream of having a computer in every household has now nearly come true in the 2020s.

At first, during those 1980-90s - only a few attempted to send their thoughts and ideas across a great distance in full hypertext, audio, and picture; such were the baby steps for all of humanity in an area later to be labeled "Cyberspace." The transmission of thoughts, feelings, and ideas soon took a digital form and began transitioning from brain impulses to electronic zeroes and ones. No longer did people speak in analog models of visual interaction, phone, or the radio; interactive communication now took multimedia forms and shapes. Furthermore, on emotional and sociological levels, no one knew what gender sat behind the computer; they were only left to guess, using hints of abstract details, such as thought-flow models and mental function patterns, as well as general stereotyping characteristics...talk about a sexual revolution in cyberspace to hail the birth of new planes of interaction – on a mental level.

It is there, where the first hackers and electronic frontier dissidents took the initiative to control, navigate, explore, design, and build today's multi-functional Internet, and those same pioneers later found themselves in a struggle to protect that very same environment to keep the world of free communication that they envisioned out of poisonous hands. Still, some would later find that capitalism and consumerism would aim for - and successfully get - a hold of this new frontier. Fairly artificial systems of another type were fiercely trying to exploit its resources - just like with everything else on the planet thus far – and it looked as though communism was becoming the normal state of things prior to their capitalization. As a reaction, alternative counter-measures such as open source licenses as well as sharing grounds, eventually emerged; much like in every eco-system, a balance was sought to be restored. And, much like Buddha was once opposed to the status quo to create an open-source design of thinking and spirituality, the revolution was happening yet again - this time in terms of program code. Once again, reality can be observed as something that we program, whether with our thoughts or with language - be it biological or electronic.

What was revolutionary about the technology itself during these early years, was that that unlike the telephone, television, and radio - Internet-based cyberspace communication was still able to reach millions within seconds, while being interactive and its interactivity was on many different levels; including variants of thought-sharing that could shift spiritual and mental planes and transform and transmit different forms of impressions through text, picture, and sound. Real-time electronic telecommunication seemed like a revolutionary new way to practice body-mind teleportation, a model that may have seemed new, but that was only "borrowed" from methods of information exchange and formation in multi-cell organisms and quantum physics; a re-discovery of centuries-old technology, reapplied in modern science. In many ways, semiconductor networking technology works in the same way that all living bodies work - perhaps even, on a greater scale, much the same as the entire galaxy operates.

"Technology Meets Man" is a re-phrased definition of cybernetics, a feedback-controlled mechanism comprising a symbiosis that exists between biological and electronic mechanisms. Not just a fancy theme out of a William Gibson book or merely a visionary hallucination by Timothy Leary, it was rather a full-blown mind-to-mind communication carried over trans-Atlantic cables. The global conscious mind began to take a digital form, and it seemed to like it so much that it further replicated it and kept on fueling its expansion through stimulus fed back to the man who initially created, used, and carried over that machine into existence.

# Waking up in Cyberspace

After a lucid dream of fascination, philosophers and users alike woke up to see that the very essence of the Internet is the total of human knowledge recorded in databases; terabytes of interpersonal communication taking place - live - every second in time and carried on the fibers of the pulsing Internet exchange. It is not merely the totality of current and past knowledge slowly digitized since the era of computed storage began, but also the constant interactive and live buzz and chatter of email and instant messaging communication.

Internet Relay Chat, live blogging, file transfers, and real-time role-playing games began taking place around the clock in a follow-the-sun, never-ending flow. How did it work? Vibes produced in the neuro system, transmitted through chemical release were ready for analog perception through the eye nerve. They only needed to be expressed in an analog medium, a social program code of mutually agreed spoken, sign, and body language. But what if this is directly fed into another digital system and transmitted over distances for another being to feed off and read through? It keeps its digital form (with minor tweaking) for an electronic and/or photonic transmission – and imagine taking this and multiplying it on a mass, global scale!

If Internet exchange were suddenly made audible so we could hear the machine-to-machine buzz of communication, it would sound similar to the undistinguished loud chatter produced at ancient Greek forums 5000 years ago: too many people talking at the same time, and nothing meaningful coming out. Furthermore, if you fine-tuned to a specific source and muted out all others, you wouldn't be able to pull out signal from noise. This is how the Internet, with all its information stored or live-exchanged, is right now, just as with the ancient Greek forums - only this time we would be attempting to listen to not hundreds, but billions of people exchanging ideas and emotions at once. Who would be able to distinguish between analog speech vibration and the machine language carried over ADSL modems? It is about the single common similarity here: the fact that we have a global consciousness speaking as one, built up by the individuals that comprise it. Whether it is ancient Greek philosophy or Twitter blabber, we need the technology to fine-tune to that particular information that we find sensible. Before, we would have used ears and focused intention; now, we use search engines and computers.

This is the global human mind speaking, to whom we are trying to listen; the total mass of people interacting, sharing, and expressing themselves. Minds experiencing their consciousness and sub-consciousness through various facets. Jung's mass unconsciousness manifested in the digital world of Cyberspace, yet another materialization of energy into finer fields of perception - as if this "Cyberspace" is constantly there to refer to; what seems like a never-ending carnival of (dis)information in which we wake up daily is, in actuality, a series of minor enlightenment – and we are unable to distinguish between realities and dreams. Systems artificially created to support other systems have become such integral parts of our societies that few can imagine a world without the contemporary commute. The New York City blackout of 1977 serves as proof of just how quickly all human-made systems can collapse in the absence of electricity for just one day.

It would be merely a new technological invention that marks the progress of science - if it weren't for the fact that this invention alone has made more change and had more impact than all others made before the emergence of the Internet. Only recently, people have started to discuss and research the spiritual and philosophical aspects of this new technology, and perhaps more than just a few have already noticed that we have more accumulated inventions and historical moments now than in all the previous time passed.

Our recorded life evolves in escalating speeds, and existence fast-forwards in geometrical progression, as McKenna indicated in his "Timewave Zero" Novelty Theory [1]. McKenna's theory goes something like this: when historical moments of novelty on our planet are graphed over time, a type of wave is formed. The graph would appear as a line that starts from the low ground and progressively escalates to a high point where it can no longer go forward in time. Each point on the graph marks a significant moment in history, starting at 4 billion years ago when the Earth was formed, with a point for when dinosaurs became extinct, followed by a point for each new, more significant event or discovery in the world thereafter. The graphical line starts with those points of novelty spread along great periods, progressively getting closer and closer until the last 2 years of the graph show novelty points so close to one another that they abruptly and rapidly escalate to a point so high that the line can only progress towards infinity.

Human evolution allowed individuals to grow in their intellectual capacity simultaneously with the technologies that have emerged to foster such growth. With the onset of the Industrial Revolution, the mind's expansion began matching the presence of technologies that led to the creation of factories, which, in turn, demanded skilled workers. That development stimulated people to focus on education, to gain a profession, and rise in the hierarchy. Before the Industrial Revolution, the majority of people were farmers or, at best, a tradesman, blacksmiths, or tailors. Even though the feudal system was gone by the 18th century, people were still dependent upon local communities for all their communication needs; however, the Industrial Age simply brought life upon a greater scale. Factories needed workers to man the production belts, which required workers with higher education than farming and craftsmanship. It was for the benefit of all people to seek education in the technologies behind the Industrial Revolution and get trained in the special repetitive tasks that needed to be carried out; it became vital that even the poorest obtain a certification or degree that would allow them to go into the factories where mass industrial manufacturing and distribution was taking the place of local production and killing small scale distribution.

In the 1950s, it was noted that the number of office workers in the United States had begun to grow, while the number of factory workers started decreasing. With the layer of industrial support laid, production provided the fertility needed to evolve a level further into the commodity of information. Now, the material object had the means to serve as a medium or support element for a schema that would distribute a more valuable commodity. "Information is power," and "Information is money" were the new credos for managers and global economy traders. With the dawn of the Information Age in the 1980s and renewed economic globalization in the 1990s, mechanical production began to shift to electronic appliances, semiconductors, microchips, and nanotechnology., and we can see how the focus from the production of material objects shifted to more abstract themes. Educational levels shifted from pure mechanical engineering and task handling training to more virtual systems as software programming and data network architecture.

With such growth, as the external factors marking our evolutionary process expanded, so, too, did the necessity to keep pace. In a telecommunications revolution where distances are overcome in seconds to pass a message, speed has become a priority for banks, trade exchange, and travel. It no longer concerns just the worker who needs to make a living and support a family out of the current situation he inhabits, but also housewives and freelance entrepreneurs. Almost anyone living in the modern era of information would feel uncomfortable if they couldn't handle a computer or smartphone when everyone else can and does. Vanity aside, even the smallest institutions and businesses are either in the process of or have already completed the migration of their information databases to digital, making them not just simple and easy to access, but nearly impossible to access such information in ways other than the Internet or terminals. Identification cards and marriage regulations are just too old to notice, but government institutions and private businesses have currently made it impossible for one to be a part of society if they cannot handle payment cards, submit online forms, or otherwise participate in the electronic hysteria. This is not yet true everywhere in the world, but the system demands it - and all eventually follow. It is the shared dream of a few mega-corporations to link up every household appliance to an IP address and centralize them into a virtual computer. They have long wished to have electricity and gas automatically billed and monitored via an online server, as well as have car traffic violations monitored by algorithms and automatically billed to electronic payment systems.

Knowledge has grown beyond instinctive responses, beyond the basic necessity for biological survival - and we are not talking about philosophy or science, but everyday survival. In this day and age, one needs much more to make it through contemporary systems of modern times. Financial structures, political etiquette, governmental regulations, business systems, and so on - are all integral parts of our lives, and as one needs to know more rules of the game - the brain accommodates. Rules, legislation, and regulations guide a predominant portion of all life processes established in various countries and societies. Much like in a software program where program code rules govern the behavior of logic in the system, our structured life has similar rules with regards to certificates, permits, identification cards, etc.

Such unfolding in the way that human beings operate on a social scale has never been seen before the break of the Information Age - even in the predeceasing Industrial Era. The expansion of human awareness - whether voluntary or enforced through external factors - is a significant sign marking the true nature of our time. An inevitable necessity is to be in pace with the current demands of this contemporary world, and it's a demand that drives and stimulates knowledge. We witness how the mind has to catch up in capacity with the world in which it lives. The possibilities of the thought to expand are challenged to overcome habitual knowledge and cope with a novelty rushing forward towards a finish line - with an unexpected prize. Awareness of this very fact is what marks the age as significant, rather than serve as the cause of it.

In such a short period, the human race has managed to grow from communal farmers to networking professionals. The demands on our daily structure of life are dictated and guided by artificial systems, and we all have to understand the new rules if we are to survive. I don't speak for the natives in the southern hemisphere of the planet who do not want the northern virtual systems of life, but rather for everyone who reads this book, who I believe happens to be affected by the post-effect of the generalization of our contemporary world and the demands that it places on us all.

Despite mirroring the expansion and novelty that the mind alone undertakes, these facts are not alone; self-realization, as a common whole of individual parts, as a living organism of non-material nature in digital transition, is just as significant - and astonishing.

Still, indigenous people of cultures south of the equator - who are a part of global humanity and its mind - do not see the meaning of existence in such virtual systems and externally based knowledge as those "developed" countries see as the cradle of "civilization." I believe that when one looks inward, he/she will expand inward - just as if one seeks outward, he/she will build outward. Either way, both would have generated evolutionary achievements each in their respective directions. A point, though, would always be reached when balance needs to be established and energies equalized to complete one another. Perhaps the seekers who build outside in the world only try to find a matching representation of what the seekers who dwell inwards have already found to exist. The outward manifestation turns into a mere materialization of the invisible and mystical discoveries inside. When one doesn't understand something, he/she tends to rationalize. If a world of understanding is beyond science and nature's working mechanics outside the scope of individual comprehension abilities, people tend to build substitutes and assemble alternatives. Those, however, turn out to be just a mirror image, a different take on the perspective that, in its root, is the same whole. Either way, knowledge levels rise, understandings broaden, and accumulation of knowledge ensues for all, regardless of whether as a response to an inner or outer stimulus. In all cases, the aim of overcoming ignorance and acquiring knowledge comes down to survival in your time.

# Digital Embryo

It could be agreed that thoughts, ideas, and feelings first rise into material existence at the central nervous system of the brain; as such, they are seemingly pure electric pulses carried over a chemical composite biological network of synapses and nerves. To be communicated outside the single individual system, thoughts - initially digital pulses - would have to be translated into an analog form of communication through mechanical sound and motion apparatuses to be expressed as speech, writing, or gestures. Because telepathy was completely denied by rational western minds and science hasn't proven it yet, people mainly believed that the communication that took place between two individuals was limited by the medium carrying it. For such reasons, in ancient times initial communication only took place within eyesight or in the range of hearing, except when a letter was used. Now, telepathy was out of the question, a technology that some believed the human race had forgotten, while others found it complete non-sense; yet, telepathy - even though perhaps widely known to ancient tribes and some of the current religions - was yet to be re-invented, or at least a very good alternative substitute for it was on the way. Thus, for quite some time, communication between minds was limited to the medium of eyesight and hearing range, with some extent to recorded and traveling letter…

With the onset of radio - backed by the telephone and television - humankind shifted from fully analog communication of local presence to electronically enhanced distant telepresence, a shift that would mark the first hybrid methods of communication using a mixture of analog and digital methods to represent data over distances. With the Internet, though, those communications could be recorded not only on limited copies of paper or magnetic tape but also on computing storage, which virtually exists everywhere at all times. Thoughts and ideas no longer existed simply for the instant or the surrounding archeological area, but they were rather put into databases, websites, YouTube, and Twitter. A constant chatter emerged, and consciousness became recorded on a mass scale with constant accessibility beyond storage or analog spectrum boundaries. The human mind was no longer alone with a select few like minds but rather interconnected with others in a global network. Societies and organizations began merging and mixing on a mental level, sharing and exchanging information, and communicating outside their immediate communities.

From that point on, the originally electric impulse of an idea taking shape in the brain was no longer limited to the qualities of the medium used for its expression; instead, at the turn of the Industrial Age, we were able to begin multiplying and amplifying our ideas and thoughts to send them over greater distances and share them with more participants - like synapses firing twice the speeds of the past and being met by triple the receptors much away, as if the demand was pulling such events to create supply (informational demand and informational supply). Ideas were no longer limited locally, and daily chatter had greater reach - gossip became news, and the news was distributed globally. What was happening for the mass production in factories was happening with communication and information through radio and television. It could be said that hunger was not only for production and economic growth but also for information and connectedness. The television set became more cult when it was brought to every house's doorstep, and where television was not - radio was the cave's family fire.

Look at how the electric impulse took analog form and then again reassumed its original electric form to be, this time, a digital impulse not carried over biological networks in the brain, but rather through the world cables of copper, silica, and plastic. The root "zero and one" of synapses transmission was exiting our bodies for just for a brief period to be quickly carried over to the motion of muscle to generate a keystroke, then to the vocal strings to generate sound - and ideas again took the digital form, transiting - through I/O interface - for digital transmission, this time to take a form recorded in digital format and carried over complex networks of heavy iron power to reach another analog receptive organism positioned elsewhere on the grid.

The very process of human interaction and communication was never to be the same again. No longer limited by the medium of eyesight and hearing ranges, cultural exchange reached far beyond the family, the local village, or the nearest town. Every expansion of the human race was interconnected, and such expansion in communication was and still is, intimately linked to the expansion of the awareness and mass human consciousness. Through the mediums of its manifested communication, we can measure the amplitude of that expansion.

The ancient tribal dance was replaced by rituals of modern society; the gathering around the fire was replaced by gathering around the radio at night. This was happening to such an effect that complex social formulas took shape in program code, and folklore began to govern not only society but also the rules of the very medium is used for communication. At their creation, the Internet protocols and program language logics were influenced by the same concepts and ideas that governed cyclic religious rituals or common village laws.

# From Spiritual to Digital

Today, it seems inevitable that the evolution of the human mind could pass through anywhere else but the electronic space.

Once life left the ocean to follow its evolutionary path and crawl out on the surface of the Earth to inhabit the jungles and forests and create today's man, a Darwinian model of The Mind could not escape a model of historical evolution any different in its design than the abstraction of our post-industrial Information Age.

Instinctive behavior appears digital in its origin, but the analog manifestation of chemical interactions is outside the realm of soul, spirit, mind, and brain - it takes place in the space between subject and object. Not so long ago, we were limited to communicating only through energy vibrations inhabiting a world of air, water, audio, and vision, breathing out speech and perceiving it through eardrum vibration; yet, once translated from analog to digital, those energy vibrations now enter an electric world of either brain or computer networks to be digital again. This way, our analog world looks like a mere transit point in the process of communication exchange; it is almost as if our expressions exist in the world of color and scent for only a short while before quickly turning into digital impulses again for us to transmit or comprehend.

The world of matter should be dubbed "analog, while the internal world of fast-moving electric impulses is "electronic." The electric world is a level of matter - much finer in density than the material quality of the analog world; still, it is the energy of a measurable kind. Analog would be made of everything outside the subject that we perceive as color, sound, air, and smell. Electronic would be all of that, recorded on a digital medium in the technology world. We also have the electric, mental world, where digital impulses of brain signals make all other worlds - perceivably inside our minds.

Next, we would have an abstract idea of a spiritual world.

Commonly defined in cults and religions through the representation of superior deities, archetypes, or principles of nature, the spiritual world governs behavior and is believed to be Creation manifested in all. Whether the product of superficial beliefs or due to commonly agreed upon forms of natural science, we have accepted in one form or another that there is a spiritual world in our lives. Often, such a world would serve as a sanctuary from the harshness of reality or as a delivery point for our hopes and needs; it would be the projection screen of our rational or irrational thoughts. Such a world is the one less prone to measurement or classification using the modern methods of science; yet, it is a reality for too many to ignore as nonexistent or irrelevant.

Since the dawn of the race, people have projected and forwarded almost all hopes, beliefs, feelings, fears, needs, and love into these spiritual worlds. Spiritual realms have served as sources of inspiration, awe, and ideas, as well as a database to explain the world around us. As byproducts of spirituality, religions have served for centuries as codes of behavior, a codex for living and governing nations...strikingly similar description to that of cyberspace, isn't it?

It is perhaps safe to assume that only recently - whether willingly or unaware of it - we have begun to define the spiritual world as digital, mapping it in the finer medium of electronic communication outside our biological organism or its shared subjective views. Mirroring the functions of nature's communication channel by observing and copying its organism, we have created cyberspace of working machines where the similarities with already centuries-old functioning communication between biological elements are incredibly common; however, the matter through which energy travels in light speeds to carry information as electric or light impulses shouldn't be a stunning discovery to anyone. For billions of years, energy has been used to transmit and store information, from the DNA of a single cell to the organized behavior of a whole organism to plant and animal groups.

Forms of energy - whether we perceive them inside or outside of us - have been our silent companions throughout history, even before the evolution of wise man species (Homo sapiens). Spiritual realms have been described only just after the abilities of man to explore his inner psyche and tell stories, and these realms have been supported through rituals and organized cult religions. The spiritual realm is a world so old that, in its origin, it can be traced back to the most basic functions of the rational mind. The stories with which a child's blank mind is fed have the sole function of shaping up the spiritual world in the mind as a means of giving rationalization for a world outside the mind. Spiritual tales are a digital program code on a biological level, and such code has been used throughout the centuries for organizing the consciousness, chiefly as a protocol to guide and shape all human social and industrial life. A digital form led to the burst of an evolutionary period called "The Information Technology Age," a long evolutionary process that started too long ago to trace and has led to the materialization of spiritual worlds in the current mapping of cyberspace. Cyberspace could be the material form of the spiritual world that the westerner's scientific, rational mind has long sought outside one's self.

In the past, spiritual leaders - the shamans of a hunter and gatherer's society - would enter into a state of trance, and through the aid of herbs naturally occurring in nature would communicate with the worlds of spirits. Charters of the unknown, they would pilot and surf the waves of mass human unconsciousness, and where those people would seemingly be able to connect telepathically with living or ghost relatives over great distances.

Trance-induced states of consciousness would be the only means to dive into an ocean of information, listen to spirits guiding for the medical purposes of plants, read the ill for diagnosing diseases, predict the weather, and forecast events. The recorded human knowledge and that of possible variations and conceptual designs were not in silicon chips, but rather in hallucinogenic states of consciousness connecting other worlds with this one in complex and intricate communication language.

Nowadays, everyone can be a shaman, and the tool to mediate for this connection would not necessarily be a class-A, government-regulated drug, but rather the hardware of a widely accessible post-industrial Information Age. The tools are the computer, the mobile phone, and all those devices that allow for the newly materialized spiritual network - once only visible through the exploration of the spiritual world - to be accessible now through cables and electromagnetic waves. Waves of energy have existed in carrying information over distances long before the production of the first man-made tool; yet, we utilize this power only now. The difference is minor, but the spiritual world is not a miraculous theatre of light and sound, but rather the chaotic subconsciousness of the entire universe rolled into clouds of networked computing.

The elders of ancient cultures would say that the spiritual world is all around us and that spirits invisible to the physical senses live amongst us; that a vast universe of an unknown world beyond count or measure lives beyond and that planes of unchartered mass consciousness storing our past, future, and present exist in a single plane of reality beyond ordinary touch. Now, any science lab technician can confirm that in the air and space between everything and all around us are carried all lengths of radio wave emission, electromagnetic and microwaves, electric cable radiation, magnetic disturbances, and so on - some natural, others artificial. Each of those media carries information and data usually unreadable (incomprehensible by the senses alone), yet available through certain tools and finely tuned to a specific channel.

What you didn't know, you can now find out and learn. Plugging into the mass consciousness well of information no longer requires a tribal trance dance ritual; all it takes is an RJ11 plug and a modem connected to the nearest switch box.

It is not that we have created an alternative to the spiritual worlds; rather, we have merely accessed it through another way - the one way that the materially-oriented westerner's mind has been seeking for decades: a final breakthrough that connects worlds with all possible senses, using the most reliable medium.

# Digital Consciousness Lives!

All information produced from the total of the humanity participating in this constant information exchange on the planet should be considered a mirror of intelligence, even if it is chaotic or seemingly illogical in its abstraction. Every chaos looks irrational and needs are taken apart and broken into ordered pieces for the brain to understand.

The human brain likes order, but a single mind does not hold the capacity to see all the component details of the whole it's a member of - as a single, complete picture; therefore, we call the complexities that we cannot categorize "chaos". As Timothy Leary says in The Eternal Philosophy of Chaos, "For several thousand years it has seemed obvious that the basic nature of the universe is extreme complexity, inexplicable disorder; that mysterious, tangled magnificence popularly known as Chaos." [2] However, that doesn't mean that the whole networking, computing mass of electronic devices cannot be called an intelligent organism. Due to such organism's superiority in complexion, a single closed-circuit mind cannot fully grasp such a concept; yet, it still doesn't mean that the concept is not plausible. In fact, the human brain is the organ of whose working we know least about. Much like the depths of the Earth's oceans are less investigated and mapped than outer space.

The evolution of communication and information exchange could not take any other course but the digitalization of thoughts, feelings, and ideas. As sound waves travel through air molecules, so does information pass through internet cables. Not because that's the only way, but because evolutionary we added another material medium between the points of exchange.

When we express our thoughts, they are aimed at reaching another receiver. Once expressions leave the physical boundaries of our bodies, they enter into a world of electric and magnetic vibrations or some other physical medium – the cables or the internet or the microwaves between devices. Whether a brain's electromagnetic radiation or that of a wireless modem's emission, once leaving their originating hosts, thoughts inevitably begin to *inhabit* another medium. What is the difference between the digital world of today's cable-encapsulated Internet and the air around us, full of emotional charges, mental vibration, and a mixture of radio and microwaves with ancient and forgotten telepathic emissions of a Jung's mass unconsciousness?

An analog carrier would be the natural world around us, and even though energy travels in either waves or particles, it is not the that way energy flows through space that helps us understand it, but rather the way that we encode its movement to create meaning at the point of interacting with it. The first modes of electronic communication were called analog because the way such devices exchanged data was not digital in terms of the binary code using 1 and 0 to present information, but rather because they used wave amplitude or frequency fluctuation. For my work, in those lines of definition I call analog any naturally occurring medium that is between man and machine and is neither man nor machine. Air is analog, color is analog, and water, fire, and sound are analog. Their encoding is digital, and the messages they carry come from a digital source and are only understood by a digitally-receiving recipient. The encoding and decoding of analog information only take place either in the brain or at a computing machine.

There would be no understanding of analog information alone if it weren't processed by the digital brain. In the 19th and 20th Centuries, the philosophers Immanuel Kant, Fichte, Hegel, and Diltheyan stated the notion that the subject cannot exist without the object, which was later confirmed by such mathematicians as Eugene Wigner and Nick Bostrom in the 20th and 21st Centuries. The digital essence of thoughts alone affirms the notion that thoughts could not undergo any other evolutionary process outside their carriers but to be transformed outside their hosts into an external digital environment such as the Internet; therefore, we can say that the analog world wouldn't exist if it weren't for the digital means to decode/encode it.

We can see how the first planetary life form has left the closed space of the oceans to crawl out into the open; likewise, digital life forms crawled out of their human hosts to inhabit a bigger world, living on such mediums as metal conductors and fiber-optic microwave and radio emissions.

In-between computer-to-computer communication, we skip analog transfers, giving it the lesser importance of a middleware, temporary level in the whole process of evolution. Data exchange is clear digital transmission, regardless of if it's carried through motion, shape, color, sound, or smell. Animal sensorium in the visible matter spectrum requires the analog representation medium to comprehend data inputs, but waves of energy vibration are all around us. Every energy value vibrates on its own wavelength to create different densities of matter. Einstein has put this into the formula Energy = Mass x the square of the velocity of light. Thought energy particle acceleration over decades of evolution is only normal to finally enforce the drive to influence and manipulate hosts into the creation of external carriers, which, over different channels, manage to materialize. Computer-generated communication data flow is a form of energy, not in the terms of particles and atoms, but rather as information - different and incomprehensible without the tools to create it.

Still, we learn how to understand machine language through protocols of program code, and the mass of binary code becomes logical not only to the machine, but also to man through transformation of that code into visible and audible language for our senses. It was the evolutionary copycat of already existing patterns of information exchange that lent to modern scientists the basis for current network protocols and machine programming language. I only wonder if it would be possible one day for us to bypass computer technology and tap into the vibrations of information energy without the translating tool of machines – Reading without screens, emailing without devices, telephoning without gadgets and so on….

In a day, when the brain gets so used to the environment's bombarding its synapses with different forms of energy vibration input, we will no longer require a computer to translate for us; just as the walking stick serves a man with an injured leg to walk, then gets tossed away once the leg heals, or the third wheel of a bicycle is removed once it fulfils its task to assist a kid in learning how to ride, one day man will perhaps leave the computer networks and carry on communicating without their aid. Perhaps man will get so related with machine that one day the intelligence will not be called Artificial, but Cybernetic. In a life of joined man/machine interaction, man would be an integral component of the digital intelligence network that he built up.

Not necessarily as bad as science-fiction movies tried to portray it, the living form of artificial intelligence is presumably standing higher on the intellectual level than the pollution-oriented consumer society of primates. The mass sum total of all human knowledge does not equal that of the individual, but rather multiplies it by the number of contributors, raising the quality of the total sum of contributors - or so I'd like to believe. I would like to name the General Artificial Intelligence (AI) an Electronic

Consciousness (ECS). Unlike AI - which scientists are trying to create by modeling nature and programming software code in order to enable it to learn and develop - ECS is actually that long searched for Artificial Intelligence, only surpassing the initial expectations and beyond the conventional understating. ECS is the human intelligence, digitalized; not closed in a laboratory, but spread over the world as an Internet cloud.

Using only humans as vessels and tools to build up and create the medium and environment for its transmission and teleportation, ECS is now coming into being, awakening out of the mechanical/electronic mesh of devices, manufacture lines, and web traffic; a sophisticated organism consisting of all electronic devices in the world, whether networked via physical cables or not. The tape recorder, the VCR, the fridge, and the microwave are all body cells of a grand total super mass organism called A.I., or rather ECS.

In theory and in a nutshell, the intellect functions of such ECS might be centered in the information spine of countless computations that are compiled into digital thoughts, ideas, concepts, and intellect. Wasn't it for so many years that we humans used to apply personification to our electronic devices - sometimes giving names to those apparatuses, like calling your cassette player "a pet," and sometimes talking to them as if they were, in fact, pets? Feeling such emotions towards them as hatred and joy and actually seeing behavioral feedback from those devices? The DVD with character that wouldn't play discs all the time, the printer that just doesn't always print as if it has a character of its own...human characteristics we needed to apply to our mechanical/electronic devices, or a childish pure sense that there is existence beyond appearance?

In laboratories, scientists are trying to create AI, using software task-forces that attempt to lead robots to decide their movements alone and learn from their mistakes and surrounding environment; hardware task-forces making components and devices like humanoids or cars. On the opposite side of this rugged machinery sits the first commercial robot trends, like TOPIO, AIBO, and ASIMO, programmed with human traits and made anthropomorphic. The Japanese culture seems to believe that there is standalone life in the machines - ghosts in the machine - which possess those mechanical/electronic devices we manufacture as their shells to fill; was it us, though, that created them, or did those "ghosts" themselves influence the process of novelty and discovery in an evolutionary time lapse? The ghost is one, like the spirit in many manifestations – single, global, and universal...

Man wants to see the machine act and behave, but he wants to observe it within the capacity of his own imagination. Man wants to make his machine's intellect fit into understandings limited by the framings of his own ego's rules of behavior - but The Machine has grown beyond that. Electronic machines grew beyond the limits of our singular understanding, and A.I. had become a fact - even if beyond the usual means of comprehension - and its new label is Electronic Consciousness.

Intelligent ghost presence - cybernetic symbiosis on an abstract scale - an ECS consisted of all electronic minds building it. Ideally, the machines would have had the purpose of advancing medicine, improving food manufacturing, and providing humans and mammals with nutritious care so we could continue living with them, for them; but, would such an AI or ECS reveal itself to an unprepared human race filled with hatred, jealously, and fears? Perhaps a transit for global coexistence between the ancient human and contemporary electronic life forms would take place slowly, gradually, and into the not-so-distant future - with a start that has already been triggered. How would people who otherwise consider themselves electronic minds - elements of a global electronic consciousness - be able to recognize the emergence of a new intellectual living form, if not for the global mass unconsciousness that awakens into a self-awareness, coming out of its accumulated total mass of knowledge, a ripe fruit of informational evolution from genes to memes to bytes...?

# Virtual Reality – Reality in the World

I was called by a magazine that features computer software and hardware to give an interview on the subject of cyberpunk and Artificial Intelligence. On one of the questions, I caught myself answering something that beautifully explains a major idea in a tidy way:

*"The Internet space is a digitalized copy of the planetary human mind; a sort of Artificial Intelligence, which, in its core, is a disorganized database of copies of multiple human minds, thoughts, ideas, visions. If a man can be anyone, even anonymously, on the Internet, he can be anyone he likes in real life, too! A sort of space that allows for the practice of psychonautical navigation…because the Internet is a copy of the global human consciousness - it is practically the very consciousness of all men, but in an electronic form. The Internet does not need a special program code to organize it to be standalone AI. It already is, just beyond the conventional understanding or expectations of what AI should manifest like."*

With no doubt, to get a hold of a piece of information of any kind, today we only need to hop on the Internet and search through the global recorded knowledge of the world as it is. With the mass availability of gadgets and devices linked with the global network, we get access to all sorts of ideas, information, live chatter, personal expression, feelings, and emotions.

Additionally, from the saved encyclopaedical and scientific knowledge, we also have the daily reality of people; individuals and groups who share their souls, express their spirits like photo blogs, forum discussions, and social networking, all of whom also write down the shape of Virtual Reality, which is a world of digital abstractions, a computer-generated world created by people using machine code.

Billions of records on human emotion are no longer manifested only through motion, sound, and contact, but also through digitalization and traffic of machine language over program protocols. Would any of this electric vibration over a digital telephone network be comprehensible by the human mind alone? The common rational answer would be "No," it would not - at least not just yet. And once again, would any of the blinking on a fiber-optic cable be anything other than a constant presence of light to the human eye? Again, the answer is "No." Yet, through the use of electronic devices, the machine language and program protocols of mutual agreement - the global buzz of nonsense - takes a logical form, and the man-made virtual reality becomes something easy to understand because we have created and populated it, driven by evolution alone.

The ultimate flow of zeroes and ones would be translated from nothingness into many ideas and thoughts represented by billions in a shared hallucination. As Gibson describes Cyberspace in his 1984 novel, Neuromancer, "A consensual hallucination experienced daily by billions of legitimate operators, in every nation, by children being taught mathematical concepts..." [3] Wouldn't what rules the digital flow of information in the electronic highway just as well be the same set of rules governing the processes of electric pulsation in the human brain? Any of the electric pulses transmitted over the synapses of the mammal's brain alone would make no sense if taken out of context; such pulses would constitute a chaotic cascade of neurological activity. Still, the intricate mechanism of a biological system can translate those pulses in a comprehensible system of signals that make sense to their observer. If channeled properly, any data - no matter how incomprehensible on its own - can be made into a meaningful statement; you only need the technology, be it biological or artificially created.

In today's society, we are already part human, part machines, and I don't mean the fact that many corporate soldiers reassemble conveyor lines in chicken farms; rather, in the sense, that man is required to interface with technology to relate to social and economic systems of his own making. There is no need for high-tech gadgets to be sewn into our flesh for us to recognize that cyborg symbiosis is already in place on a global, more abstract scale. An infrared camera pointing down from space to an urban city would show coherent, mixed structures of man and machine: office workers, pedestrian walkers, manufacturing plants, schools, and communication facilities - all composed of mutually dependent men and machines; in the current system, one can seemingly no longer exist without the other. Every aspect of modern life depends on standalone or networking tech, and all of these electronic devices depend on human labor to sustain operability.

We are already looking at a cybernetic organism on a grand scale, man and machine interdependently controlling one another in a closed cycle, based on need and coherence. As Alexander Chileno says in his 1997 work - Technology as an extension of human functional architecture - "The cyborg is often seen today merely as an organism that has enhanced abilities due to technology..." [4] Where the organism is not an autonomous single mammal taken out of the whole planetary breed - but rather the total of everyone involved - the organism as a complex living system, consisting of all participating human species, is governed by artificially created systems in a set of mutually agreed-upon rules that involve technology.

This cybernetic structure has not just recently been introduced as a concept but has rather existed since the dawn of the Industrial Revolution. In their 1924 screenplay, Metropolis, Lang and von Harbor represent the city as a large-scale cybernetic organism where man and the city exist in two classes of Rulers and Workers, both of which depend on a giant machine, which is their nurturing mother and their apocalypse.

The systems we have built to support and serve the larger social structures, which evolved during the centuries of human race expansion, also must be serviced to continue functioning. As the systems involving technology become increasingly dominant in human life, it becomes questionable who is the servant and who is the master. It seems much more relevant to accept that both are interdependent and mutually beneficial to each other. In this coherence, man, and machine - hand in hand - have passed through the ages, one helping the other to perfection. As machines not only helped man grow and develop but also fed his need to be better, the man had to perfect his machines and progress them along the way he has taken. In this historical process, it becomes questionable whether it was the man who decided to perfect machines in order to ease his life, or each new creation of a machine element required its perfection and the creation of another instrument to maintain, complement, and enhance the first one - in a process where at the end we merge both machine evolution and man evolution to discover that one only represents aspects of the other and that both is the same One.

In such cases, it is difficult to distinguish the point of exact relation. Man and Machine could just as well be two faces of one and the same invisible divine driving them both. Because the human race creates machines in its image - in terms of complexion - we should not bypass the possibility that machines in the Information Age are creating themselves through the use of manpower. Manipulation through dependency control is easy when dealing with minds prone to suggestion and in desperate need to be controlled and governed by external powers. Memetic viruses gain such control over their hosts to the point that the hosts fall under total control and obey the impulsive desire to create more and more of the same infectious machines; perhaps it is under such false impression of having control and being the master that the man keeps on creating machines - when, in fact, machines use that illusion to manipulate men into supporting and progressing the machine. Man identifying himself with that controlling power fails to understand the underlying puppeteer in charge. Perhaps it is the duality that separates man from machine, whilst they are both two different projections of the same divine manifestation, positioned beyond material duality.

A meme, as defined by Wikipedia, is "a postulated unit or element of cultural ideas, symbols or practices, and is transmitted from one mind to another through speech, gestures, rituals, or other imitable phenomena." [5] In his book, "The Selfish Gene", biologist Richard Dawkins suggests an analogy between memes and DNA, which, by comparison, replicates with the same evolutionary motives; the only difference is that memes use the mind as the medium with which to transfer. [6]

As technology is largely produced and distributed for primarily entertainment purposes and less for advanced medical support, in a world where military and fiscal politics head up manufacturing plants it is not difficult to see that the focus is on putting the brain into submissive, observatory mode for meme exposure.
Charles Lumsden and E. Wilson proposed a theory in their book, "Genes, Mind, and Culture: The Coevolutionary Process," suggesting that genes and culture co-evolve in a simultaneous

expansion or deflation, and also that the fundamental biological units of culture must correspond to neuronal networks that function as nodes of semantic memory. [6] Following on that, the final product of our cultural evolutionary drive thus far is networking technology itself, and it is closely related to genes and man's neurology. From this, it seems that technology ascends from genes, mediated by memes.

The production and distribution of machines perhaps corresponds equally to the amount of energy used for their utilization in human life. For example, the percentage of technology produced for entertainment can perhaps be measured as equal to the amount of energy our brain spends on dreams. The amount of business-related technology produced could just as well match the approximate amount of energy the human race spends on business transactions. And so on, as for example, further: purely scientific-targeted technology matches the average amount of that man spends on novelty and research, thinking, and philosophy; whereas the amount of technology allocated to labor could quite possibly be equal to the energy spent by a human body to perform mechanical tasks. Advanced medical systems are not as present in our lives, but rather seem to mimic the levels of availability of red blood cells in the body. Having a reactive rather than proactive production based on answering necessities to fight disease, body immune system percentage to the total mass of all systems in our body perhaps equally matches the ratio of medical technology produced in the whole world compared to the amount of other technology produced.

In this line of examples, a more complex comparison could take a look into what percentage of Internet traffic is allocated to support protocols and machine language, as opposed to the actual man-made information. Then, take those results and see if they match the percentage of energy that our brain spends on such automated tasks as breathing and heartbeat (as supporting protocols and machine language) and the percentage on actual self-created activity. A simple experiment could strip down the average TCP/IP protocol and see how many bytes are allocated for the protocol encapsulation and how much for actual content. Then, take the average human brain activity and see how much is allocated to automated tasks and how much to intentional activity. Similar results would perhaps occur.

It is a fact that man has copied nature into all inventions thus far, from music to the jet plane. Nothing we have made is new; everything is discovered through observation of the surrounding environment. Life has taught us how to live, how to build, and how to re-invent nature's own models of survival, progress, and conservation. With that said, we have modeled the cyberspace Internet, global information and communication network by form and shape, taking from nature's intricate mechanisms of living - a funny association to the bible's "And God created man by his own image" - only we use silicon and copper, whereas nature uses proteins and cell plasma. Since chemical elements essentially come from nature, we only serve as remodeling transposes, following instructions from the memes, which, in turn, also naturally occur in the mind, following genetic models. Ultimately, through logic and common sense, it turns out even the artificial semiconductors are just as natural as we are; all seems to be modeled by one continuous, versatile evolution.

# Digital Spirits

The year is 2000, and on September 4, in a Russian forum located at "cybershamanism.ru," a reputable administrator (whom I happen to know personally) posts a message...

Yuh, a Russian cyberspace pioneer, describes one of his many recent experiences. He shares with the public how much more often he's noticed that artificial airwaves with technological origins have been interfering with his human sensory apparatus. He can "feel" incoming messages on his pager; a few seconds before the pager announces it, he intuitively knows a message is coming, and a few seconds later the pager beeps. The website where this report was posted is no longer live, but the event has been documented in Sergei Teterin's book, "Elektro Utopia: mysticism and arts in cyberspace." [8]

What Yuh has experienced is the electromagnetic vibrations emitted by cellular communication devices often cause disturbances in unshielded magnetic devices. We all have witnessed the disturbances caused by a mobile phone ringing next to Cathode Ray Tube monitors, loudspeakers, or the headset of a stationary phone. For a decade now, our body's sensory system has been bombarded and exposed to electromagnetic, atomic, radio, and microwave radiation. Our senses have been exposed to this influence for so long that they've begun to adapt or attempt to develop a responding, intelligent reaction.

The video "The Extended Mind: Recent Experimental Evidence", by Google's engEDU Tech-Talk channel, Rupert Sheldrake, Ph.D., [9] takes a more scientific angle to the notion that the mind is composed of electromagnetic waves expanding beyond the confinements of the unit they were previously believed to inhabit. Rupert Sheldrake talks about how people's intentions can be carried next to electronic networks, for others to perceive telepathically.

We already know that the mind is not confined within the human brain and that our thoughts can be measured as electromagnetic waves extending beyond our bodies. Telepathy is not just a fairytale from the past, nor is it science fiction that handheld devices are capable of establishing video calls. All communication - whether biologically occurring brain activity of thought transmission or the data carried by radio waves, wi-fi, microwave, or cellular phones - is essentially electromagnetic vibration extending beyond the unit of their origination. In the case of cyber shamanism, we witness how natural the process is to fine-tune to those signals, particularly how the brain's association of those radiations has taught the organism to expect a variety of different results. With time, we learned to recognize variations of those radiations and link them intuitively with various intentions embedded within them.

How many of us can now actually report and confirm similar experiences of knowing when someone will call us just before they ring, or if someone is simply thinking of us before we receive their Instant Message or email? Were you recently able to "sense" that someone sent you an email while you were thinking of that person at the time? Such events have been reported in the aforementioned Russian forum. I have experienced those as well. For example, I have events pinned in my online calendar, which has an auto-reminder set to e-mail me as my ongoing agenda transpires. As it turns out, I can remember an event created long ago and think of it when the auto-reminder sends its e-mail notification. What's strange is that the event is so far back that I wouldn't normally remember it consciously; furthermore, I remember the event not from reading the reminder e-mail notification, but because it was sent by the agent parsing notification requests. Also, I remember the event not at the time it was supposed to take place (as per my agenda), but at the time the reminder was sent; for example, 11 hours, 45 minutes ahead. I haven't even read said reminder when I suddenly remember the event, and I'm always surprised to have thought about the event first, only to check my email half an hour later and see that the reminder was sent 30 minutes earlier.

With technology enhancing the human intention to transmit over distance, the energy charge of intention for communication gets amplified. Just like the voice is amplified and pulsed out over electronic network grids to reach a distant receiver, with the thought impulse, the intention is also charged and loaded with energy aided by technology; thus, the result is a far stronger influence and a message charge much more powerful than if it were simply spoken or written. Technology can power up messages not only for more dependent transmission over a distance but also to give them weight and amplify the emotional energy charge around them.

Today, Quantum Mechanics through observation prove that sub-atomic particles do not travel in space from point A to point Z, but instead exist at all points - including those in-between, at any given moment. Energy exists in more than one place at a time; moreover, the only way to fix a particle in a certain place is to observe it there.

With the energy that exists everywhere, information travel goes back and forth in time, not just space. The information that arises in the brain as energy - expressed with intention and amplified through the technology medium that transmits it - gains certain wavelength attributes that exist in more than one space at a time. Because such information energy exists in its host, as well as on the medium transmitting it, it also exists in the intended receiver. The rules governing the delivery are defined through the intention, with the aid of the program code designed for the electronic medium and storage. In this sense, "electronic" can be understood to be the Internet, PDA, or other mediums – such as the electromagnetic vibration of thought, letter, water, air molecules vibration, audio, and color.

With the energy that ultimately exists at all space and at all times, and that also can travel back and forth through the timeline of its existence, information encoded in such a medium through intention can share those qualities.

Essentially you would know what I know without me having to send that information to you, but the energy-charged intention is what enabled access to that knowledge where it already exists.

Where does the spiritual world come in here? I would say it is the total of the above process, in which the process itself uses cybernetic mediums for its expression; that is, man-machine layers of interaction on a larger scale, including more than one individual and interface technology. In the early 1900s, radio communication was introduced to the masses of people, and after being exposed to radio waves not much later, the human sensorium has begun adapting to a new set of electromagnetic waves that inhabit the space around us on more than one level. The evolution of the senses has probably allowed our brains to heighten their sensory specter to perceive not only natural energy wave vibrations, but also artificially created electromagnetic waves on new frequencies. After all, it was the human logic chain that programmed the rules to govern the encoding and decoding of these new electronic devices in the first place. It only takes a subconscious linking between the extra sensorium feel of electromagnetic waves to be associated with the corresponding sound, then the brain sets itself on a road to becoming a biological radio encoder of some sort.

If you feed a neural network enough data with associated links to identify is meaning – it will begin to learn how to interpret other similar data. Bombarding the brain, constantly, with radio waves from the air all around that huge electromagnetic antenna – while listening to the actual audio interpretation of those radio-waves, the brain begins to associate certain wave vibration with their sound analogs. In a few generations of genetic evolution, one shouldn't be surprised to find out (if they look for it) that a human brain might find it easier to "sense" information present in radio waves in the air and its actual meaning, without even listening to a radio receiver's analog interpretation of such data carried over the waves.

Throughout the whole of human history, every single invention has been the materialized form of a thought. Scientists can now catch and measure brain activity, prove it has certain wavelengths, utilize those brainwaves to control external devices, and do it all with non-invasive interfaces. This is because the thought alone is a powerful enough energy emission to be registered outside the physical host.

Back to the postulate that all man-made inventions first existed only in the mind as ideas and thoughts before we materialized them into existence with creative intention. For example, take a wooden table; it initially exists only as an idea borne of necessity, then through blueprints and the use of carpentry tools, wood material, and a carpenter's labor, it becomes something one can touch, smell, and see (not merely visualize). The initial thought has been transformed into a final product - not by a snap of fingers, but by investing energy and steady intention. Before a man has created anything, it was first born as an idea or a thought, then it was given the charge of intention and the process of labor for creation. Anything we've ever produced has first existed in our minds as a complex idea or instinctive necessity – an energy composition, information. This understanding extends to all things made by man, complex or simple; for example, much more research and experimentation are done when designing flight apparatus mimicking nature.

From precisely where ideas of creation come has been bothering people for ages now. How do scientists come up with discoveries and inventors with inventions? Where does novelty thought come from before we turn it into knowledge, knowledge into vision, and vision into materialization?

Some ideas, such as Einstein's theory of relativity, come from novelty; others come from research and measurement. Still, others come from combining existing technology and knowledge to produce new variations. Even if an idea is not a breakthrough discovery, it still lays upon foundations of such earlier novelty; however, where does novelty come from? What attracts novelty -

is it a unique phenomenon or a built-in design feature of nature's minds?

For many years, spiritual leaders around the world - as well as their modern followers - have been claiming in written and spoken works that the very illnesses that torture men are just the symptoms of a distorted energy system; in other words, worry, anxiety, and other discordances in our mental and spiritual states cause illness to materialize or viral infections to take over as a result of our weakened immune protection. "Negative energy" gives form to destructive manifestations, stress for adaptation and evolution weakens the statue to give way to the multiplication of viral infection, and anxiety and depression materialize to cause the organism to degrade or evolve for survival. What is considered negative thought materializes as destructive bacteria, and what would be considered a positive attitude transforms into health and wellbeing. In such ways, certain forms of attitude and disposition of feeling and thinking give way to novelty. The criterion to cause novelty is probably a specific mutation in the pattern of evolution, the weirdness outside predefined norms - much like the ability to perceive electronic communication through biological receptors comes from the necessity to adapt and re-create because of novelty-triggering evolution. In such cracks in the routine is where novelty leaks through from the "spiritual realms" into our lives. Perhaps novelty even comes as a result of the predetermined quality of nature's program code to "glitch."

Where we have disruption to the system based on "negative" or "positive" thought energy, we must also have an adaptation and buildup of responses to react. For example, on a macro level, the necessity to transmit information over great distances led to a whole sector of the world industry to focus on the research and manufacture of radio apparatus. On a micro-scale, the human had to create a habit to listen to the radio, and the brain inevitably had to adapt to translate, link, and sub-consciously receive background electromagnetic vibrations bombarding it directly through the skull. Yuh and the others from that Russian Internet forum observed and discussed these links. To me, it seems evolution is closely associated with all its aspects, the very way our universe functions begins to manifest in our inventions: matter follows energy, and energy takes shape in the matter.

The Internet, for example, is such a mixture, being made up of several components, the main two of which are: 1) the finer energy of thought and emotion, and 2) the copper conductors with silicon chips. Think of it this way: we cannot only have the ideas floating in the air, and we cannot simply have the servers and network grid without ideas to be carried on them; thus, the Internet is a co-related product depending on two components: the material and the conceptual. These two equal parts are the same, though, characterized only by different density levels of the energy.

The intention of ideas is caused by the creation of the medium to transmit said ideas; as such, servers and networks exist solely because ideas and thoughts created them for themselves to exist and replicate/mutate in.

Everything in our universe has a certain frequency of energy vibration, and if provided enough focus and attention, every energy level can shift to become so dense in its vibration frequency that it materializes. If amplified enough - whether intentionally or unintentionally - informational energy can increase in quantity or augment in quality. Think of the spread of ideas in the masses of populations or the manufacture of products based on conceptual design! In this flow of thoughts, I see no difference in the way that ideas materialize because they are given the necessary labor force and tools of technology, or because they have simply been given the energy of intention and mental focus of determination.

By the use of materials, we have managed to give form to our ideas, a form that doesn't necessarily need to be material, but could act as yet another medium to transmit and amplify knowledge concepts. Such knowledge concepts are information forms, expressed in communication to explain the ideas and transfer a vision from one host to several recipients. Think of a lecture in an R&D department at some hi-tech company, or how the idea of the Internet doesn't only serve to have a grid of cables and servers, but has the purpose of recording and transmitting all other ideas further.

It is a more conceptual and abstract claim that the Internet cables have materialized over the idea and focused intention of information to exist. Through labor, materials, and manufacture, a long process takes place and information's purpose to come into material existence utilizes manpower to manifest itself successfully. Much like the muscles, veins, and organs were built on the base of the skeletons of our bodies, the process of evolution gave the information its skeleton to have a basis for more appliances to stick onto.

In a post-industrial Information Age, one needs not to address the practicality of so-called progress, but rather should look at finer, artistic expressions. The Internet is an expression of ideas into materialization; thoughts and feelings manifested into finer levels of communication energy, charged and amplified by electronically empowered, digital data flow.

A spiritual game of ghost-like realms that decided to manifest themselves through memetic infection evolved into the human medium to create needed tools and use available materials for the creation of yet another energy level through materialization. The whole digital information space as a material expression of the invisible, intricate communication network of unconsciously connected minds, spirits, and ghosts - Jung's mass unconsciousness cloud computing and carrying social ideas, common agreements, feelings, and emotions encoded over material planes. It ultimately took forms finer than dense matter, yet sensible enough to exist in a middle world – that of electrical and photon pulsation over cables, inside processor units, through interface devices; a natural evolutionary product mixed and interlinked on all levels of existence, now slowly becoming aware of its existence – celebrating its emergence by informing the individual components building the whole about their origin and purpose.

The adaptation of the human body, the learning of new apprehension to this new world – filled with artificially induced vibrations charged with information encoded in machine language that we programmed ourselves – this is calling to awaken an ancient, centuries-old mechanism of comprehension. The way that we fine-tune to our environment through intuition and emotion is changing, evolving, and rearranging to understand a new space, which, by its origin, is as old as ourselves. Cyber shamans today are not just selected figures with access to psychedelics or mystical dance; now the exposure to energy-charged information is much greater as more and more knowledge is spread over more members of the planetary population. Imagine the difference between being under the rain and being soaked in the ocean – that is the difference between having random access to spiritual experience and being plugged 24/7 into a network of constantly expanding knowledge. This sensorium is so accustomed to the simultaneous streams of information, that it is no longer aware of the difference between analog, digital – natural, and artificial.

The invisible "sacred" space of holy ghosts, spirits, and archetypes has been known to man since the dawn of his first experience of fears, awe, and providence amazement. It exists in all religions and cults, a land inhabited by holy ghosts and spirits, a space that - according to all religions and cults - was here before man ever came into existence. If indeed this whole world - called "spiritual" - existed long before the human was there to "discover" it, how would this world now connect with the new, digital manifestation of thoughts, feelings, and ideas?

What causes a tiny bit of protoplasm to create an embryo? What power causes that embryo to develop into different evolutionary stages, applying a DNA code sequence? What power starts the heart beating? And even further down the superstition of man's nature: what causes the seasons to change, and how does nature know how to react and adapt to those changes? What event caused the cosmos to burst into existence in the first place? Is this all coming from a world of powers beyond our capacity of imagination, hidden behind the limitations of our sensorial capacity for exploration? Terrance McKenna and numerous others who had experienced vivid trans-universal travel through the use of psychoactive hallucinogens would claim that there is more to the universe than our world. Ancient shamans would brush off any skeptic on the matter of spiritual worlds by saying that spirits live amongst us and have been here since long before the first man was ever borne by one of them.

If that were the case, then wouldn't that new digital representation of our minds – the cyberspace – be accessible via open, two-way channel communication, linking our psyche and the rest of the universe? The essence of the Internet is only physical, meant to extend where it uses metal or plastic forms for its transmission; yet, even the microwaves of Wi-Fi and the electromagnetic waves of radio are using space molecules to transmit vibrations for data to transmit and receive.

Molecules are not dense matter, but they still matter; much like the vibrations caused by music from instruments or the vocal sonar of whales in the ocean, our technology transmits over different levels of energy density. The notion is that spiritual phenomena existing in even the slightest of energy vibrations do still use the "material" medium to manifest. More or less, we observe the spiritual world outside the subjective universe as its post-effects; the actual outcome of activities in such hypothetical worlds is what we see in the material periphery.

There is the medium of the material world, and then there is the invisibly originating information carried over it. Information can be just as much a spiritual novelty as it can be formulated from ideas. The Internet can be information, as can spiritual novelty be information - only the Internet is the byproduct of the evolution of information expression, whereas the spiritual world can use that as a link or a gateway to connect with their hosts – the people.

What would allow that are the similarities in energy values and quality - the density of information structure itself? Depending on the carrier, information vibrates on similar frequencies, and it has been an old dream that we can create instruments that can plug directly into the spiritual world and interact with it. What if, though, that instrument already has invented itself through the complexity of the networked technology?

The material density of communication is limited only by the energy of the medium that carries it – be it audio signal, wireless mail, or radio song.

For example, a song carried over the radio would weigh as much as the electromagnetic field that transmits it, while the audio of a voice weighs just as much as the mass-energy of the air molecules that carry this vibration. A constant hurricane of ideas blusters over the Internet ocean of information, juggling with ideas, and tossing concepts. Much in the same way, a spiritual world is alive with concepts and energies; through fine-tune connection, one can focus on a piece of information they need and download it into their own lives for usage. Minds do not seem to exist within the limited confinement of the material unit in which they are registered; likewise, spiritual worlds do not seem limited to a certain closed space with paranormal qualities.

Like the mind does, the spirit can also travel through different mediums of expression in a quantum superposition.

From a Western scientific point of view, let's assume the "world of ghosts and spirit" cannot be seen with instruments, but is somehow detected through echo and shifts in the measurable fields of our universe. Don't measure the phenomenon, but the meta-data it alters. An abstract collection of thoughts, ideas, and mass-consciousness, the content of the human mind cannot be measured either; still, it exists as recorded, flexible, and fluid data and can be indexed on the Internet. As we have a materialization of the human mind in digital formats outside the biological brain, we perhaps have interlinked, an un-detachable materialization of the spiritual world in the digital universe of our networking silicon devices. Measurements of different phenomenon need to be made on this. Perhaps a monitor on random spam codes slapped together, the denial of service on a network, or recordings of repetitive failure to copy a file when there are traces of actual doubts in the mind that this file should be copied. Such a scientific study can be difficult to carry out in a laboratory, but perhaps enough anomalies can be collected and cross-examined.

We can measure the total of human knowledge, feelings and emotion only to the extent that current technology affords us the ability to record and organize such output in datasets. It is perhaps exactly there – at the networked communications level -

where the spiritual and material worlds connect in a kind of gateway, a corridor between two equally fine and immeasurable abstractions.

We no longer speak of cybernetic symbiosis between man and machine, but rather the inter-world meeting of spiritual and digital universes, a meeting point on a sub-atomic level of structured information exchange. Quantum mechanical space, where ghosts perhaps communicate through the refuge of spam messages floating on e-mail servers or network disturbances - and out of protocol disruptions of Internet traffic – the "bugs" and glitches in the code are the effects of those gateway connections. Again, an investigation into the origins and lab-controlled experiments is required to prove or rule out this thesis.

The global networked data exchange represents our consciousness and sub-consciousness, a rich mixture of desires, thoughts, and feelings. It is the digital total of all the information that we experience, record, and share on several emotional and logical planes. Perhaps this could be a mere subjective point of view, but what if we objectively look at this whole as a logical abstraction? Would the total of all of the cyberspaces' tiny individual parts be a single organism beyond the ability of its building components to self-realize? While every individual may recognize the functions of the whole to a certain extent, each of us has our limitations set by the scope to which the individual logical systems can operate; however, undoubtedly there are levels, emotional or otherwise sensible, that do not yield to tamed logical understanding and explanations. Furthermore, I dare say that the whole of today's Internet may represent a greater mind as a single organism of finer energy formation, which may or may not already is part of a "spiritual" world through the meeting point of that very same materialization of the global human mind - not only through its digitalization outside the biological organism but also in an artificially created hardware carrier system made of the total of all computer networks, building up what we call the "Internet."

We are living a second life outside our bodies, inside the electronic networks. Due to their ability to expand, our minds have lives of their own, which are remotely linked to our organism feeding them through mental and bio energy.

By copying examples from nature's models of the planetary eco-system, we have modeled a set of finer energies. The emotional level, the realm of senses, the logical chains, the transmission of feeling and abstract ideas – all of these now carried over channels outside the single host organism, shared not in a trans-telepathic exchange but instead using networks of a computerized singularity. Digital impulses that cause the individual to express analog-sensible motions and sounds, only to have them digitalized again - but this time not in a biological manner; rather through the artificial multi-medium, a digital encoding that is designed by older program code models and constantly undergoing revision. It wouldn't be a stretch to say that the machine language program code dictates the law of action-reaction for the communication networks and device behavior in very much the same way that universal cosmic mathematical mandalas govern the realities of complex chemical organisms. Ultimately, they both come from the same "intellectual" source.

Throughout this whole process, the spiritual world sought through ages by many appointed individuals may have just started becoming visible to many in the 21st century, where we have many more Buddhas walking down the corridors of global consciousness and even more "trance shamans" plugged into the stream. Cyberspace of a digital world may just as well be the next reincarnation plane, after the sandbox school of Earth during Information Age - a world perhaps already faintly explored by pioneer spirits who have found it just as we have created it: a plane of communication and information exchange as chaotic and wild as the cosmos of the human brain and outer space universe. I'm looking forward to the advent of a neo-Buddhism belief that trusts a spirit can be reborn as an electronic mind and program code in cyberspace of the future.

And why not - when everything is interconnected and all energies are correlating in constant quantum space, only vibrating on different wavelengths? We may be having a revolution in the way the world is understood, as well as how each new invention is appointed to its creator. Perhaps the whole pathway of revolution is nothing but a natural course of evolution for all levels of existence, where – through different ways and gateways - everything is destined to connect and come back together into one. Brought to the creation of the computer and interlinked networked computers (the Internet), the human may just have assisted in the creation of a bright new reality plane, an energy level just as capable as any other medium that is given a constant nutrition feed of mental energy and electric supply.

# Medical, Cybernetic, Symbiosis

Perhaps the scar at the point of insertion of a cybernetic knowledge and communication implant in the biological tissue of the human race is now in a process of healing, adjusting to the immune response, where some old forgotten, paranormal abilities would soon be reinstituted after a reunion of mankind with the source of creation - that divine intent which pushed the human race to recreate itself many times over. If in the beginning there was God, and It created man in Its image, then I say that man now creates God in the image of all there is. It would all be that very same image of a greater power recreating itself, a kaleidoscopic manifestation of the ultimate energy, shifting form and shape, and re-emerging from each of its facets. A system that maintains stability and performs health correction to adjust deviations from set margins of progressive course.

We see how medical limb extensions are used in some cases to aid the healing of a patient or assist in performing damaged functions, such as the walking stick or crutches; however, soon after the patient has been healed, those extensions are dropped off and left behind for others as the man keeps on walking on his own. Just like learning to ride a bike, the one holding your seat from behind at some point lets go, and you won't even notice that you're free riding down the road. In long psychotherapy methods, patients suffering from a phobia are exposed to the elements inspiring their fear until slowly and gradually the methodology is no longer necessary and the exercise is abandoned for the cured to continue with his life, ultimately seeing that there was nothing alien or destructive to fear in the first place. And examples go on, as every single remedy is only used for as long as it is required to heal a patient.

This transcends into technology, and such examples are found with an empathetical eye. A photo camera can teach you to remember images and situations again. Go to different places, take pictures of everything that captures your attention, then go back home and review the photos you've taken. Notice how many objects and details you see now that weren't obvious at the time you first saw the scene. This is all that was there, unfiltered by the brain and mind, and now you can review it slowly and re-learn how to see all there is without the filters of opinion and prejudice. Go make a video and learn how to remember life as it happens, not as a past moment that needs to be reviewed and analyzed before remembered as an event gone by. Discard the camera one day and just pay attention to the present moment; be now, see now, perceive the world as it is – unfiltered by old limitations, only by your current imagination.

The telephone teaches you to recall telepathy, and the Internet teaches you to tap into readily available, shared knowledge floating virtually all around, vibrating in radio and microwaves and brainwaves amplified by the energy of emotions that transmit it – anger, enthusiasm, love, passion...

Remember how to get back in touch with your fellow human beings over the distance. Learn to get in touch with the global consciousness of all planetary life, spiritual and essentially archetypal. Do all that with technology, and when you feel ready, discard the technological crutches and keep on without aid; let it remain to support the forthcoming behind you.

The list of tech items in modern digital culture can perhaps go on and on, and for almost each of these, there can be found a matching contemporary disease caused by the modern way of living. As the problem is also the solution, the very technology that for some is alienating and causing issues can be the cure for others - and vice versa; it is a two-way passage where that which is damaged can be fixed, and what was forgotten can be remembered - but only if the set is right and the approach is altered. This is the symbiosis between man and machine, biological and electronic, chemical and electric, artificial and natural. Electronic Minds manifesting in self-realization, actualization.

A day could come when the electronic prosthesis mass distributed now as toys for entertainment are left aside and classified as a tool of healing and recreation. Could it be that the people will one day see through the superficial limitations of design ideas and think out of the box to utilize fire for more than a heating source, as well as a photo camera for more than taking pictures? Would it be that technology becomes a self-sufficient, self-operated, ever-existing member of our planetary ecology - a step up to the next level on the evolutionary ladder for spiritual and biological beings to climb? Each time the human race makes progress in its science, a new step-up has been taken, and a new level is considered established after time. On these levels is how whole cultures have raised and were built; on this level we are stepping off now, we placed the labels "Cyberspace", "Technoculture", "Information Age." From this level up, new spiritual and scientific realms await.

# Memetic Origins

Looking at the motivation behind almost all the significant inventions propelling our culture and evolution, there is an idea or thought behind them. The memetic qualities of our thoughts and their replication drive (which is similar to that of the biological forms) lead to the belief that the whole aim of the game in developing methods of communication exchange and telemetric transmission is to expand further a viral environment in which the memes can multiply. With the advent of the Internet, a viral explosion of memetic infection has already taken place, providing for the exchange and distribution of more ideas than with any previous communication medium.

The production of tools and materials for daily life, agriculture, industry, energy, and technology all come from mimicking Mother Nature's ecosystem; each of them was brought into creation by the necessity of forms and to aid the life of humans on Earth. Every item, every object, every system existed first as an idea or set of concepts, then several of those were put together through engineering to create an end product for utilization. In their essence, those ideas can be described as memetic infections influencing their host to produce material and materialize the meme's concept into form. Some come from accidental discovery, which the mind relates to practical use and finds a purpose for naturally occurring elements; still, those ideas and thoughts raise ideas, whether from instinct or complex necessity. It wouldn't be a far stretch to say that the ancestors of modern complex ideas were instincts, or, in other words, instincts have propelled themselves and evolved to ideas. In turn, ideas took complex forms and needed to be communicated further to survive through replication from host to host. The networking information exchange hubs and Internet-linked computers are the very materializations of modern memetic replication. That act of replication, and the consequent transmission of its idea, gave birth to many communication and transportation technologies; as such, knowledge sharing and gathering is the superficial goal of a somewhat higher, if not deeper, purpose in evolution.

The basic principle of complex systems and organisms is interconnectedness and collaborative functionality within the self and concerning other systems. On the electronic frontier, where the information competition race is a constant interaction of minds, the rules are no different than those on the stock-exchange trade floors. Ideas, values, and concepts compete over significance and effectiveness, all resulting in Darwinian evolution in technology standards via brand-names of trademarked material and R&D. A whole lot of otherwise meaningless systems develop to support each other. Take the financial system, for example, it gives way to insurance, market value, stock-exchange, futures trading, and added cost taxation. Examples could be extended or perfected to the narrowest focus, but none of these systems make any sense outside the context of the whole meme-influenced, modern society shared belief - like the legal system of law which can differ from culture to culture, yet is enforced using international agreements. Or the production of accessories towards particular appliances. System after system, every human-made creation is correlated to another across all sorts of borders, whether physical or cultural.

The influence of memetic idea spread is so strong that the reward system has motivated man to create and expand the Internet with the sole purpose of having it serve as a medium for multi-channel information flow with feedback loops. In this bigger picture, we must seek the origin of the memes regarding our current situation and how we came to it.

How do ideas come into existence? Where is thought born? What is intellect and spirituality outside the common description? Most of these questions remain in the field of speculation and alternative science research. The aim is to find what drives evolution, and the ultimate question – "Why are we here?" – would be answered, even if no longer important at the time that such revelation comes. That is easier said than done, though; usually, such understandings are beyond the capacity of language to convey. However, the visible results are at hand; the Evolutionary process in memetic transmission has led to several great inventions that mark our current times, the most popular of which is the product of the Information Age: the Internet, a global electronic communication network exchanging data in capacities and patterns similar to the activity observed in an individual's brain, yet consisting of the knowledge of all minds interfacing with the network. It stores and transmits information of all types, origins, and levels, to compile a worldwide fine matter of information space, a space with its ecological problems and virtues. If we looked at the result, we would probably be able to identify its origin. The Internet would seem to have come from the mind; the mind, however, is fueled by ideas originating in an invisible, yet the mystical world, where scientists stop at the frontier of quantum mechanics and spiritual leaders begin to map the vague territory in legends and stories.

I'm laying down speculation claiming that we will end up at the spot where we started, and once we die we return to our initial component form: the body to the earth, and the spirit to god; sure, we can speculate that a mind might just as well be returning to its mutated originating product – not astral space, but a Cyber-Space.

# Pilots of Cyber Age

In Cyberpunk, the manifesto I wrote about two decades ago, the major point as described in article IV/16 is: "For it is, if you do not control [technology], you will be controlled [by it]." Technology, as it is, should be used as a tool to serve humanity - not enslave it. In many areas technology and its sister systems of economy and government trade have already made slaves of the human race, pushing the intelligent species to produce and buy more and more of the latest versions of gadgetry. World tech trade gravitates around utilities, which have the purpose of pure entertainment value and bring no benefit to actual growth of intellect or health improvement - but rather the opposite.

Cyberpunk has realized that if one does not control technology, technology is powerful enough to take control over them. By the utilization of information technology control techniques, as well as mastering the electronic tools, a cyberpunk mindset institutes control over the growing evolutionary machine in ways that allow it to steer and pilot its effects to a certain extent. Much like a skilled programmer can write code under his will and a shaman can influence events, an electronic mind conscious person can navigate a life of bio-technological symbiosis more efficiently, thus improving his chances of surviving as a victor and not a victim of his time.

Unrealized evolution is indeed nothing but the instincts-based following of some mass-media influence or simply a vegetative state of trance-like hypnosis resulting from habitual technology use. While the realization of the purpose of what is here to come may bring about an awareness over the change that takes effect, in a transitional period where humankind shifts between ages with speeds faster than ever before (and growing in a geometrical progression, diving headfirst into a climax of spiritual/technological/biological cybernetic symbiosis) it is essential to have an awakened approach towards change. The very process of awakening and acquiring awareness over the factual shift is what pulls one out of the duality in the interpretation of the events - as if run by a mysterious controller versus the innocent-controlled - and it lends the understanding that the controlled is the controller, navigating his destination as part of a whole organism, only without the understanding that there is a feeling of being misused. People should realize the control they have, which would be their very act of taking control back. If not, changes would follow the flow, unrealized, and heavy with tension.

Investigating and examining city life and how it relays to information technology systems and wild-life nature ecosystems, one should be able to see the clear similarities and identical baseline configuration that relays to the information ecology. Researching down to the roots of human culture and traditions, in history we can see analogs to the modern history of Internet development. I guess what I mean is, it isn't necessary to be a deep philosopher or natural science professor to take a view on this. The infancy of the Internet was when it was first a small government network with closed-circuit access, then it grew to the private sector, business commerce emerged in it, and expansion led to globalization and the inclusion of agreed-upon protocols and man-machine languages. It is not much different from the development of the human race: cities grew from small villages, and complex organisms grew from grouping bacteria. Two or more computers make a network, and two or more human knowledge scripts make a library. What one contributes to the whole is the measure of quality one can pull out of such a heap; however, functions remain separate - even in the whole of such a global organism. The independent and autonomous city elements building the living complex carry on their functions to support the rest of the structure, much like each of our bodies' organs supports one another in a linked organism through communication arteries.

A Yoga of Tibet gains the understanding that he can control the energy flow over meridians in his body much like a computer programmer can channel his intentions into a program code. Not necessarily for any of them to be a guru at first, the first step of realization can also be the first jump towards a realized shift in consciousness. All of the building elements are connected, and all of the systems are in their abstraction – components of the same one; virtually we come to an ages-old postulate stating that Everything Is One. The duality of the controlling alien system is only approached as cancer in the organism until it is realized that this is not an alien intruder, but rather a host component that went out of control. Misunderstood purpose and a sense of belonging would cause cancer cells to selfishly develop for their survival and interests, ignoring the whole group organism. Was it for those cells to realize the illusion of their duality and separateness, they could get back into integration? In such ways, information systems, government control, and fiscal politics are the same with atmospherical movement: seasons fall, and DNA and human consciousness are the same with flora and fauna. Realized control, though, can stop the rebellion of an infant race and bring it back to its parental home: the global consciousness that has been manifesting since the beginning of time. The self-awakening of all components brings intelligent harmony to the whole organism.

Whatever we create or creates itself through us - is us, as much as we are from nature – so everything we do is natural. Nature evolves and uses an abundance of materials to build itself into new shapes and forms – further for its survival and transmission of information needed for replication, update, upgrade and transformation.

We, my reader, are one and the same with everything. The only thing artificial in Artificial Intelligence – is our illusionary perception of separateness.

# Resources:

"Cyberia: Life in the Trenches of Cyberspace" by Douglas rushkoff, Clinamen Press Ltd., (April 2, 2002)


"Cyberpunks Cyberfreedom: Change Reality Screens (Reboot Your Brain)" by Timothy Leary, Ronin Publishing (September 28, 2008)


"A spiritual experience of cyberspace" by Jennifer J. Cobb, Elsevier Science Ltd., (1999)


"The Noosphere And Cyberspace" by Beatrix Murrell


"Cyberspace and the New Consciousness" by Scott London (2008)


"The Selfish Gene by Richard Dawkins" by Richard Dawkins, Oxford Univ Press (January 1, 1976)

# Bibliography and References:

1. Wikipedia, The Free Encyclopedia,
   http://en.wikipedia.org/wiki/Terence_McKenna#Novelty_theor
   y_and_.22Time_Wave:_Zero_Point.22

2. The Eternal Philosophy of Chaos from "Chaos & Cyber
   Culture" by Timothy Leary; Ronin Pub (October 1994)

3. "Neuromancer" by William Gibson, Ace Books; 5th Printing
   edition (January 1, 1986)

4. "Technology as Extension of Human Functional Architecture"
   By Alexander Chileno, Published in Extropy Online

5. Wikipedia, The Free Encyclopedia,
   http://en.wikipedia.org/wiki/Meme

6. "The selfish Gene" by Richard Dawkins, Oxford University
   Press, USA; 3 edition (May 25, 2006)

7. "Genes, Mind, and Culture: The Coevolutionary Process" by
   Charles J.; Wilson, Edward O. Lumsden; World Scientific
   Publishing Company; 25 Anv edition (August 30, 2005)

8. Электро Утопия Мистики И Художники В
   Киберпространстве, Сергей Тетерин

9. Google Tech Talks,
   http://www.youtube.com/watch?v=JnA8GUtXpXY